Cycle
Northumberland

routes for people

Published by Sustrans
National Cycle Network Centre
2 Cathedral Square
College Green
Bristol BS1 5DD

Tel: 0845 113 0065

First published 2004 by Sustrans (registered charity no: 326550).
Maps based on Ordnance Survey Strategi and OSCAR digital data with permission
of the Controller of Her Majesty's Stationery Office.
© Crown copyright. Licence no: GD03181G0001.

ISBN: 1-901389-45-6

Produced by Cycle City Guides, Wallbridge Mill, Frome.
Printed by Butler & Tanner, Frome, Somerset

Maps
Pages 17 to 78 include original field surveys by Stirling Surveys, with additional
information provided by Sustrans.
Pages 79 to 125 produced by CycleCity Guides with data supplied by Ordnance
survey.

Photographs
Cover photographs: © Steve Morgan and Alex Telfer
Pages 1, 9,13, 24, 25, 52, 61, 80, 118, 119 © Alex Telfer
and used courtesy of ONE NE Tourism team.
Pages 27, 30 Tynedale Council
All other photographs © Sustrans and Nick Cotton

Contents

Northumbria's Cycling Kingdom Rides

Day Rides

Acknowledgements

Many thanks to all of the staff at One North East Tourism Team (formerly Northumbria Tourist Board), who have been very helpful and keen to promote cycle tourism, particularly Michelle Turnbull and Katherine Hodgson (marketing, photographs), Carl Burn, Pam Pedelty and Andrew Marchbank (for providing accommodation and attractions data), Katie Lister (route surveying) and Susan Marshall.

Thanks also to the staff at Sustrans North for helping to compile data, map routes and proof read this book. Also the Staff at the National Cycle Network Centre, Sustrans Bristol, for help with all sorts of things including the content of this book (maps, text, photos) and helping to promote it. Stirling Surveys, Ordnance Survey and Cycle City Guides for the excellent mapping to be found throughout this book.

A special mention to Northumberland County Council, and other project partners, for continuing to work with Sustrans to provide better cycle routes and facilities throughout the County. Also One North East and Northumberland Strategic Partnership, for funding towards Cycle Tourism. Without this input, many of the routes described in this book would not be available.

And last, but certainly not least, the very dedicated Sustrans Volunteer Ranger, Doug Ridgway, for survey work and information on Hadrian's Cycleway.

Introduction

Welcome to Northumbria's Cycling Kingdom with wonderful rolling countryside, vast skies, quiet lanes, spectacular castles and magnificent coastline. This is a perfect area to be explored by bike.

This book describes the main touring circuit (more correctly, the triangle) made up of three National Cycle Network Routes (see map on page 8). Hadrian's Cycleway (Route 72), running west from Newcastle upon Tyne along the Tyne valley through the historic towns of Corbridge and Hexham to Haltwhistle; the Pennine Cycleway (Route 68), heading north-east from Haltwhistle to Berwick-upon-Tweed along the foothills of the Cheviots; and the Coast & Castles Cycle Route (Route 1), hugging the coast south from Berwick to Newcastle.

This guide describes this ride in a clockwise direction, starting and finishing in Newcastle. This is because the prevailing south-westerly winds are likely to be of most help on the hardest section – the Pennine Cycleway from Haltwhistle to Berwick. However, as the route is signposted in both directions, there is no reason why you should not do it anti-clockwise.

Also featured are 11 day rides starting from points on the circuit, enabling you to devise itineraries that range from a short half-day trip on a railway path to longer and tougher challenges.

How long will the whole circuit take? This is not a tough route in terms of hills, but there are several off-road sections that can't be ridden fast, particularly laden with panniers. So the superfit may do the whole loop as a challenge over three or four days, but for those of you who wish to stop and enjoy the cafes, pubs and attractions such as Hadrian's Wall and the castles down the coast, a week to 10 days would make for a more relaxing holiday.

If you only have a long weekend, there are plenty of options: you could enjoy several of the day rides, or hop on one of the fast East Coast mainline trains (or a Tyne valley train) to take you one way, or you could do a shorter loop. For example, you could just ride the top part of the triangle: either Berwick-Wooler-Belford-Berwick, or Berwick-Whittingham-(Shilbottle)-Alnmouth-Berwick.

The book is laid out so that you can easily find the information you need, whether you intend to spend a week or more on the 220-mile tour, find a route for a long weekend or try one of the many day rides.

How to get to Northumbria

Northumbria is England's North East Region and includes the counties of Northumberland, Tyne and Wear, County Durham and Tees Valley.

NATIONAL RAIL OPERATORS

An easy and effective way to visit Northumbria.

Great North Eastern Railways
08457 225225
www.gner.co.uk
National Rail Enquiries
08457 484950
www.nationalrail.co.uk
Virgin Trains   08457 222333
virgintrains.co.uk

LOCAL RAIL OPERATORS

Once in the region contact
Arriva Trains   0870 602 3322
www.rrne.co.uk
The Metro   0870 608 2608
tyneandwearmetro.co.uk/metro

COACH AND BUS

A great way to reach Northumbria and very cost-effective.
National Express Travel Enquiries
0870 808080
www.nationalexpress.com

LOCAL BUS ROUTES

Once you are here, Northumbria is well served by local bus routes. For timetable information contact
Travel Line North East
0870 608 2608
www.jplanner.org.uk

BY FERRY

Ferries link to Northumbria from Holland, Scandinavia and Germany via North Shields International Ferry Terminal. Sailings are frequent and enable overseas visitors to bring their cars and tour Northumbria at leisure!

For sailing times, prices and offers contact:
DFDS Seaways
08705 333000
dfdsseaways.co.uk
Fjordline 0191 296 1313
www.fjordline.co.uk

BY AIR

Northumbria has two international airports - Newcastle and Teesside - that handle flights into the region from UK and European airports. Contact the airports for flight information.
Newcastle International Airport
0191 286 0966
www.newcastleairport.com
Teeside International Airport
Tel: 01325 332811
www.teessideairport.com

OTHER TRAVEL INFORMATION
BY TRAIN

A minimum of 2 bikes can usually be carried on train services. Reservations are usually unnecessary on local services operated by Arriva Trains Northern (cycles are carried on a first come first served basis), but reservations are required on services operated by GNER, Virgin and other long distance services. You can make a reservation for your bike at the ticket office prior to departure or by phoning National Rail enquiries.
08457 484950

Travel within Northumberland
See page 124 and 125 or visit
www.visitnorthumbria.com

The main 220-mile circuit

The route has been broken down into stages, mostly 20-30 miles long. You may wish to do one stage a day, but this is only a suggestion – you could do more, or linger over some of the attractions en route. The stages start and finish in towns or villages where there will be a reasonable choice of accommodation and refreshments.

Ten suggested stages

Stage	Grade	Miles	Page
Newcastle to Hexham	Easy	25	14
Hexham to Haltwhistle	Moderate	23	21
Haltwhistle to Bellingham	Strenuous	28	27
Bellingham to Alwinton (or Rothbury)	Moderate/ Strenuous	22	33
Bellingham (forest route) to Alwinton	Strenuous	40	37
Alwinton (or Rothbury) to Wooler	Moderate/ Strenuous	23	43
Wooler to Berwick upon Tweed	Easy / Moderate	28	49
Berwick to Bamburgh	Easy/ Moderate	23	55
Bamburgh to Amble	Moderate	28	61
Amble to Newcastle	Moderate	40	68

Northumbria's Cycling Kingdom circuit

Signed Routes
- Coast and Castles Cycle Route 1
- Hadrian's Cycleway Route 72
- Pennine Cycleway Route 68

Unsigned Routes ● ● ● Link route

Berwick-upon-Tweed

Holy Island

Bamburgh

Belford

Wooler

Northumberland
Heritage
Coast
AONB

Whittingham

Alwinton

Shilbottle

Alnmouth

Rothbury

Amble

Northumberland
National Park

Ashington

Bellingham

Morpeth

Blyth

Tynemouth
Corbridge   Newcastle

Haltwhistle Hexham

Gateshead

Short breaks

The points of the triangle formed by Newcastle, Berwick and Haltwhistle
are all well-served by bike-friendly train services, so it would be easy to
ride one or two sides of the triangle and use the train for the third. The
other railway station with a reasonable service is Alnmouth, half way
down the coast between Berwick and Newcastle. As it is feasible to work
out a safe route on lanes to link the two sides of the circuit between
Whittingham to Alnmouth (via Shilbottle) you soon see several
possibilities for an enjoyable two- to three-day ride.

About the day rides

Northumberland has a wonderful network of quiet lanes and tracks ideal for recreational cycling. Many of these are used in the main Northumbria's Cycling Kingdom circuit, but throughout the county there are many other options for shorter, circular rides, eleven of which are described here. The rides all start from small towns or villages, enabling you to get straight out onto the lane network without needing to battle with urban traffic. Some rides may take little more than an hour, others offer half day outings if you are fit or a full day out if you are riding at a more leisurely pace, stopping to see the sights and taking refreshments at the cafes, tearooms or pubs along the way.

The start points for the Day Rides are all located on the main Northumbria's Cycling Kingdom circuit so if you want to extend your time on the circuit, you could stop at various of the bases along the way, drop your panniers at your overnight stop and explore the area more thoroughly.

Two of them - Haltwhistle & Plenmeller Common and the Rothbury ride - are only suitable for mountain bikes as they use rough tracks. The others can all be ridden on ordinary touring bikes as the short offroad sections are neither too rough nor too long.

The Day Rides are shown on Ordnance Survey Landranger mapping at a scale of 1:50,000, so 11/4 inches on the map represents one mile on the ground. The Day Rides are not waymarked hence the need for route instructions which are broken down into short numbered packages of information; the corresponding numbers on the map point to the relevant junctions on the ride. As several of the rides feature a mixture of lanes and tracks, the line on the map showing the route may cover a minor road, a stone-based track or occasionally a rougher earth track.

Holy Island

Eleven, one-day rides from seven bases

1 **HALTWHISTLE TO LAMBLEY VIADUCT** Page 78
10 miles. Easy / Moderate
On and off-road.
South Tyne Trail. Railway path / lane ride to Lambley Viaduct.

2 **HALTWHISTLE TO HADRIAN'S WALL** Page 80
7 miles. Moderate
On and off-road.
Hadrian's Wall.

3 **HALTWHISTLE TO BARDON MILL** and **PLENMELLER COMMON** Page 82
15 miles. Strenuous
On-and off-road.
Bardon Mill and Plenmeller Common.

4 **BELLINGHAM TO WARK** and **GUNNERTON** Page 86
31 miles. Moderate / Strenuous
On-road.
In and out of the North Tyne Valley to Wark and Gunnerton.

5 **ROTHBURY TO COQUETDALE** Page 92
24 miles. Strenuous
On- and off-road (mountain bikes only).
Westwards along and above Coquetdale.

6 **WHITTINGHAM TO THRUNTON WOOD** and **ABBERWICK** Page 96
17 miles. Moderate
On- and off-road.
Thrunton Wood and Abberwick.

7 **WHITTINGHAM TO GLANTON** and **INGRAM** Page 100
11 or 16 miles. Moderate
On-road.
Along the foothills of the Cheviots to the Northumberland National Park Visitor Centre at Ingram.

8 **WOOLER TO CHILLINGHAM** and **CHATTON** Page 104
22 miles. Moderate
On-road and one very short section off-road.
To Chillingham Castle and Chatton, along the valley of the River Till.

9 **KYLOE HILLS, NORTH OF BELFORD** Page 108
17 miles. Moderate
On-road.
Around the Kyloe Hills to St Cuthbert's Cave.

10 **BELFORD TO CHATTON** Page 112
27 miles. Moderate / Strenuous
On-road.
Chillingham Castle, Ros Castle and two good pubs.

11 **WARKWORTH TO DRURIDGE BAY** and **AMBLE** Page 118
11 or 18 miles. Easy
On-and off-road.
Druridge Bay and Amble.

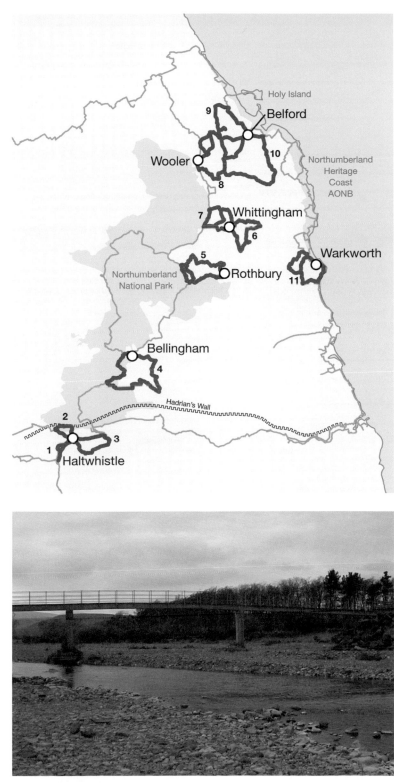

Brandon Ford near Ingram

Key to maps (pages 14 - 73)

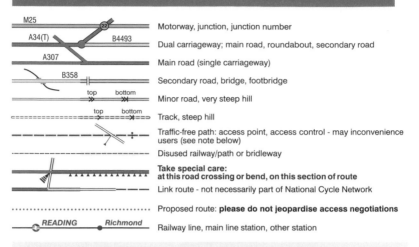

Motorway, junction, junction number

Dual carriageway; main road, roundabout, secondary road

Main road (single carriageway)

Secondary road, bridge, footbridge

Minor road, very steep hill

Track, steep hill

Traffic-free path: access point, access control - may inconvenience users (see note below)

Disused railway/path or bridleway

Take special care:
at this road crossing or bend, on this section of route

Link route - not necessarily part of National Cycle Network

Proposed route: **please do not jeopardise access negotiations**

Railway line, main line station, other station

Access controls built to restrict motor vehicles are designed to allow cycles and standard wheelchairs to pass, but may inconvenience users. As the Network develops, our aim is to see them removed. For a free copy of Sustrans' 'Removing Barriers on the National Cycle Network' information sheet please call 0845 113 0065 or visit www.sustrans.org.uk

The presentation on this map of a road, track, cyclepath or footpath is no evidence of the existence of a right of way. The National Cycle Network is measured in miles.

Distance markers at 1 mile intervals

Mileages between selected points

The Royal Bank of Scotland millennium mileposts

0 - 50m	Buildings, church
50 - 100m	Built-up-area
100 - 150m	Sea/estuary
150 - 200m	Lake/reservoir
200 - 250m	River/canal, canal bridge number
250 - 300m	Small river/stream
300 - 400m	Woodland or forest
400m +	Major cliff or quarry

Base **scale** is 1:100,000. Inset town maps are at larger scales. **North** is indicated by a blue arrow. **Distances** are shown in miles. **Heights** are shown in metres above sea level.

Travel Information - facilities on or near the route are shown by green symbols. Further information can be obtained from Tourist Information Centres; telephone numbers are listed on each panel.

🏧	Tourist information centre (open all year)	Cafe, hotel or public house
ⓘ	Tourist information centre (seasonal)	Grocery shop, cycle shop or hire
👫 ✉	Public toilets, post office	▲ Campsite
▲	Youth hostel (YHA)/independent hostel	◈ Journey record stamping point
☎	Public telephone (in rural areas only)	Nature Reserve Selected places of tourist interest
Abbey (NT)	National Trust property	

The map sections in this guide cover a wide area; however it is only in the vicinity of the route that they have been surveyed in detail. Outside this area only major features have been mapped. If you wish to travel further afield we recommend the relevant Ordnance Survey Landranger maps. Neither Sustrans nor Stirling Surveys shall be responsible or liable for any loss or damage whatsoever arising from the use of the National Cycle Network or this map.

The 220 mile circuit of Northumbria's Cycling Kingdom

Newcastle to Hexham

72 🚲 ❯
25 miles
Easy
Follow Hadrian's Cycleway, Route 72

The Northumbria Cycling Kingdom circuit can be done in either direction. Here, it is described in a clockwise direction so that the prevailing south-west wind is most likely to help on the toughest section, the Pennine Cycleway from Haltwhistle to Berwick-upon-Tweed. The first two stages, from Newcastle to Hexham and from Hexham to Haltwhistle, are the most suitable stages of the whole circuit to be ridden as self-contained day rides, as there are several stations along the way and frequent trains, enabling you to catch a train into the prevailing westerly wind and cycle back into Newcastle.

The ride starts on the Quayside in the very heart of Newcastle, using the wonderful traffic-free riverside path, with fantastic views of all the bridges above. After a mile or so you leave the river and follow urban cyclepaths to cross the Scotswood Road and join a railway path above the Tyne. A little way along the path you come across the junction of Hadrian's Way, Route 72 with the C2C (Route 14) which takes a southwesterly course up the Derwent Valley to Consett.

For Hadrian's Way, leading to Hadrian's Cycleway stay on the north side of the river, soon dropping down to the Newburn Riverside Park, which has a splendid new section of cyclepath right by the river. Suddenly you are out of the city and into the rural surroundings of Tyne Riverside Country Park. The cyclepath takes you right past the birthplace of George Stephenson, of Stephenson's Rocket fame, before following the tree-lined Wylam Waggonway. A steel Meccano-style bridge at Hagg Bank takes you over to the south side of the river until the end of the traffic-free path at Prudhoe Station, where you recross to the north bank in Ovingham, passing the tall Saxon tower of the Church of St Mary.

At this point you join the network of lanes, starting with a lovely section by the river then soon turning away through a gently undulating landscape of arable fields and copses of broadleaf trees, home to innumerable pheasants. The first busy road of the trip (the B6530) takes you into the centre of the handsome town of Corbridge, with a wide choice of excellent pubs and cafes. Four miles to the west you cross back to the south bank of the river to enter the historic town of Hexham with its magnificent abbey, where the first stage of your journey ends.

Follow Hadrian's Way through Newcastle

GRADE OF DIFFICULTY

Easy. This is the easiest stage of
the whole 220-mile circuit.

MAJOR CLIMBS

One climb of 215ft (65m) that takes
you away from the River Tyne and
into Corbridge.

PUBLIC TRANSPORT TO HEXHAM

There are regular half-hourly trains
between Newcastle and Hexham
from Monday to Saturday and
hourly trains on Sunday. Newcastle
to Hexham (and on to Haltwhistle)
is the very best section of the
whole route to use the train for a
day ride as you can travel due west
into the prevailing wind and be
blown back to Newcastle. If you get
tired you can also pick up the train
at one of the many stops along the
way to shorten the trip.

NATIONAL RAIL ENQUIRIES

08457 48 49 50

ARRIVA TRAINS NORTHERN

Customer Helpline
0870 602 3322
www.arrivatrainsnorthern.co.uk

TOURIST INFORMATION

NEWCASTLE UPON TYNE

Central Station
0191 230 0030
City Centre
0191 277 8000

PRUDHOE

01661 833144

CORBRIDGE (SEASONAL)

01434 632815

HEXHAM

01434 652220

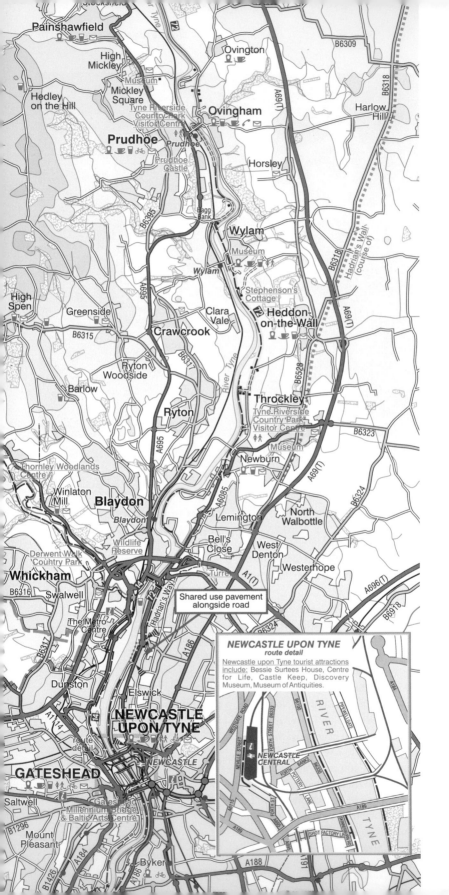

NEWCASTLE UPON TYNE
route detail

<u>Newcastle upon Tyne tourist attractions</u>
include: Bessie Surtees House, Centre
for Life, Castle Keep, Discovery
Museum, Museum of Antiquities.

Shared use pavement
alongside road

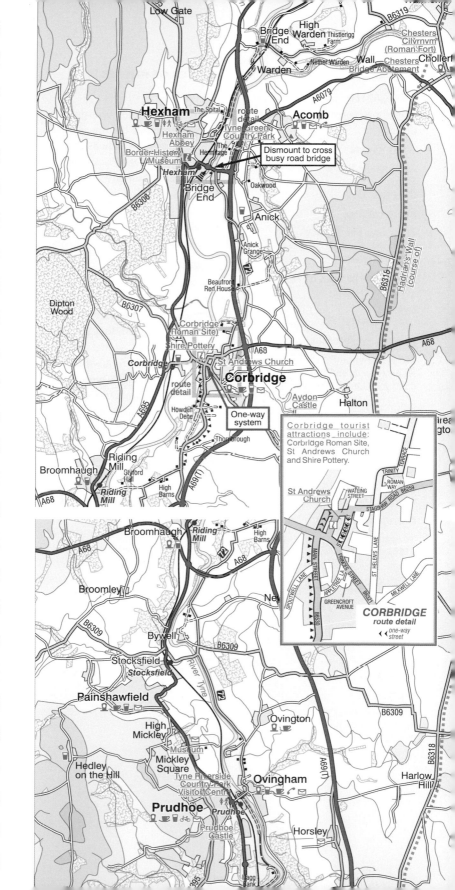

BIKE SHOPS

NEWCASTLE

Only those nearest the route are listed.

CYCLE CENTRE

250 Shields Road
Byker
0191 265 1472

CYCLE LOGICAL

37 St Georges Terrace
Jesmond
0191 281 8383

EDINBURGH BICYCLE CO-OP

5-7 Union Road
Byker
0191 265 8619

DENTON CYCLES

259 Scotswood Road
Newcastle upon Tyne
0190 232 3903 / 0191 274 9786

PRUDHOE

BICYCLE REPAIR MAN

Unit 6b
Earls Court
Low Prudhoe Ind Estate
01661 830618

ECONOMY DRIVE LTD

19 Front Street
01661 832516

CORBRIDGE

TYNE VALLEY CYCLES

The Forge, Bridge End
01434 633363

HEXHAM

THE BIKE SHOP

(Also cycle hire)
16 St Mary's Chare
01434 601032

PLACES OF INTEREST

WYLAM

The railway pioneer, George Stephenson, was born here in 1781. His name will always be associated with the Rocket, an early steam locomotive. The museum in Wylam illustrates the village's place in railway history (01661 852174). Visit Stephenson's birthplace (01661 853457).

CORBRIDGE

The information centre is located in a peel tower which was built in the 14th century to protect the vicar of the Church of St Andrew's from marauding Scots. At the nearby Roman site, built to guard the bridge over the River Tyne, are the remains of a storehouse, the largest Roman building in Britain. The museum shows the archaeological discoveries found on the site. 01434 632349

HEXHAM

St Wilfrid used stones from the nearby Roman camp of Corstopitum to build the original abbey in AD 674 and there is a stone seat in the present abbey, built in the 12th and 13th centuries, known as Wilfrid's Throne. The Moot Hall dates back to the 15th century and the old gaol, built in the 13th century, now houses the Border History Museum.
01434 652349

Alongside the Tyne In the heart of Newcastle

REFRESHMENTS

Newcastle – lots of choice

Newburn – the Boathouse Pub, at the start of Tyne Riverside Path

Between Newburn and Wylam The cafe at George Stephenson's Cottage

Wylam (just off the route) – lots of choice

Prudhoe (just off the route) - Adam and Eve Pub at Prudhoe Station

Ovingham – Riverside Inn

Ovington (just off the route) – Winships Tearoom

Corbridge - lots of choice

Hexham - lots of choice

ACCOMMODATION

NEWCASTLE

Budget option

Newcastle Youth Hostel (very keen to welcome cyclists as the hostel warden is a cyclist himself)

Newcastle Youth Hostel
107 Jesmond Road
Newcastle upon Tyne
0191 281 2570 or 0870 770 5972
email: newcastle@yha.org.uk

Medium options

Many of the City Centre 'budget' hotels such as the Travelodge, Premier Lodge have secure underground car parks where a bike could be kept.

There is a good choice of B&Bs and smaller hotels at the edge of the City - Jesmond / Sandyford

Gateshead Millennium Bridge and Newcastle Quayside

areas are a short (5-10 min) cycle ride away but accessible to the city centre attractions.
Contact Tourist Information on 0191 277 8000

Luxury option

The Malmaison on Newcastle Quayside - popular with rich cycle touring Norwegians!
Malmaison Hotel
Quayside
Newcastle Upon Tyne
0191 2455000

CORBRIDGE

THE HAYES
Newcastle Road
01434 632010
www.hayes-corbridge.co.uk

GOLDEN LION HOTEL
Hill Street
01434 632216

PRIORFIELD
Hippingstones Lane
01434 633179

RIVERSIDE GUEST HOUSE
Main Street
01434 632942
www.theriversideguesthouse.co.uk

FELLCROFT
Station Road
01434 632384
email: tove.brown@ukonline.co.uk

HEXHAM

HEXHAM YOUTH HOSTEL
YHA Acomb
Main Street, Acomb
(2 miles north of Hexham)
0870 770 5664

ALEXANDRA BED & BREAKFAST
10 Alexandra Terrace
01434 601954
www.alexandrabandb.co.uk

HIGH REINS
Leazes Lane
01434 603590
www.highreins.co.uk

WEST CLOSE HOUSE
Hextol Terrace
01434 603307

BURNCREST GUEST HOUSE
Burnland Terrace
01434 605163

DUKESLEA
32 Shaws Park Road
01434 602947

LABURNUM HOUSE
23 Leazes Crescent
01434 601828
email: laburnum.house @virgin.net

Hexham to Haltwhistle

23 miles
Moderate
Follow Hadrian's Cycleway, Route 72

Hexham Abbey

The route continues west from Hexham Tyne Green Park on a traffic-free path alongside the railway line, emerging close to the Boatside Inn in Bridge End. Just east of here the Tyne splits into two. The River South Tyne runs almost due west to Haltwhistle then turns south to its source in the Pennines just below Cross Fell; the River North Tyne heads north then northwest to Kielder Water. Hadrian's Cycleway follows the North Tyne on a northern detour, worth doing if you wish to visit the Roman cavalry fort at Chesters. Otherwise, you may prefer to avoid one of the two climbs and stay on the more direct route to Fourstones, in the valley of the South Tyne.

The fine yellow stone houses and farms in the village of Newbrough represent the start of the first long climb since leaving Newcastle. You are rewarded with excellent views south over the valley of the South Tyne to the Pennines, giving you a real idea of the vast feeling of space that characterises Northumberland. The climb is along an old Roman road, Stanegate, running parallel with Hadrian's Wall, which lies a couple of miles to the north. Shortly after the start of the fast descent, a right turn takes you around the back of the Roman fort of Vindolanda.

Just after this point, you have a choice. If you are pushing on to Bellingham, turn right shortly after Vindolanda, following the Pennine Cycleway (Route 68) to go past Once Brewed Visitor Centre and head into the wild remoteness of Wark Forest. If you are staying in or visiting Haltwhistle, turn left downhill. The slightly round-about route has been designed to give cyclists a safe subway crossing in Bardon Mill, beneath the fast and busy A69. From here, an undulating lane between the A69 to the north and the River South Tyne to the south runs into the fine little town of Haltwhistle.

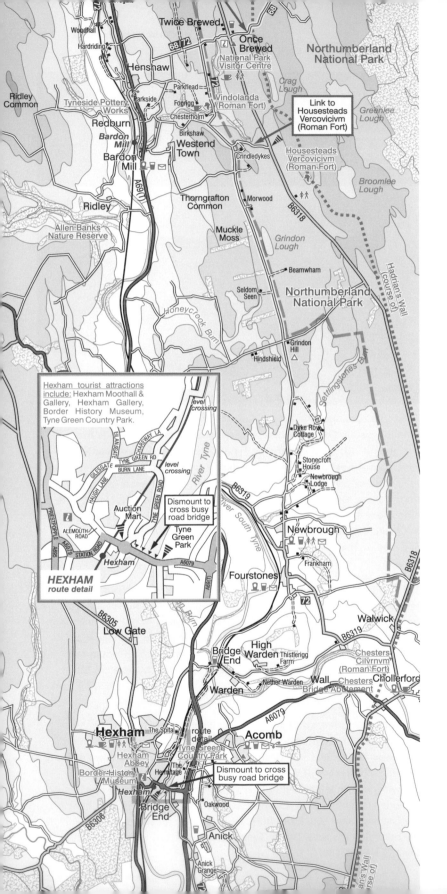

Thorngrafton Common, above Bardon Mill

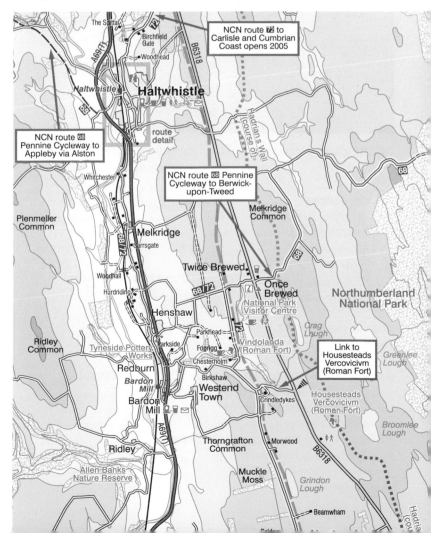

GRADE OF DIFFICULTY
Moderate

MAJOR CLIMBS
1   Two short climbs of 115ft (35m) and 165ft (50m) between Bridge End and Fourstones.
2   Longer 655ft (200m) climb west of Fourstones to the top of the ridge above Bardon Mill.

PUBLIC TRANSPORT
There are hourly trains between Newcastle and Haltwhistle throughout the week. As explained in the Newcastle to Hexham stage, this is one of the best sections of the whole 220-mile circuit to use the train, catching it westwards from Newcastle or Hexham, giving yourself a one way ride with the wind behind you.

NATIONAL RAIL ENQUIRIES
08457 48 49 50

ARRIVA TRAINS NORTHERN
Customer Helpline
0870 602 3322
Website
www.arrivatrainsnorthern.co.uk

TOURIST INFORMATION
HEXHAM
01434 652220

HALTWHISTLE
01434 322002

ONCE BREWED (seasonal)
01434 344396

BIKE SHOPS
HEXHAM
THE BIKE SHOP
16 St Mary's Chare
01434 601032

HALTWHISTLE

THE BIKE SHOP

17 Westgate
01434 322544

EDEN'S LAWN SERVICE STATION

(cycle hire and spares only)
Bypass Road
01434 320443

PLACES OF INTEREST

CHESTERS ROMAN FORT

01434 681379
(1 mile north of the route)
Remains of Roman barracks, stables
and the commandant's house can
be seen at this Roman cavalry fort,
located on Hadrian's Wall by the
banks of the North Tyne.

VINDOLANDA FORT

01434 344277
Excavations at the Roman fort have
produced a plethora of relics
including letters, boots, sandals
and jewellery, all in a remarkable
state of repair. There is a replica of
a section of Hadrian's Wall, with a
reconstructed kitchen.

HALTWHISTLE

Despite its medieval name,
Haltwhistle has a history going back
much earlier, when Ancient Britons
settled in the surrounding hills. In
the 2nd century AD the Roman
Legions arrived to defend this
northern frontier of their empire,
resulting in the construction of
Hadrian's Wall, 73 miles long from
coast to coast and now designated
a World Heritage Site. During the
bloodthirsty and lawless times of
the Border Reivers, the buildings of
the area were highly fortified and

Cycling is thirsty work

Haltwhistle boasts more 'defensible' houses than any other English town. The coming of the railway in 1840 opened up the town as a centre for mining and quarrying.

REFRESHMENTS

There are plenty of places to choose from in Hexham and Haltwhistle. In smaller villages, try:

Bridge End – Boatside Inn
Fourstones – Railway Inn
Newbrough – Red Lion pub
Vindolanda Roman Fort
  – tearooms

ACCOMMODATION

ONCE BREWED

ONCE BREWED YOUTH HOSTEL

Military Road
Bardon Mill
0870 770 5980
email: oncebrewed@yha.org.uk

BRIDGE END

BOATSIDE INN B&B

(on the route 2 miles west of Hexham)
01434 602233
www.boatsideinn.co.uk

HALTWHISTLE

CENTRE OF BRITAIN HOTEL

Main Street
01434 322422
www.centre-of-britain.org.uk

ASHCROFT GUEST HOUSE

Lanty's Lonnen
01434 320213
www.ashcroftguesthouse.freeserve.co.uk

HALL MEADOWS

Main Street
01434 321021

OAKLEY KNOWE FARM

01434 320648

GREY BULL HOTEL

Main Street
01434 321991
www.vizual4u.co.uk/greybull

Haltwhistle to Bellingham

28 miles
Strenuous
Follow Hadrian's Cycleway, Route 72
and Pennine Cycleway, Route 68

Hotbank Crags, Hadrian's Wall

This stage through Wark Forest is the most remote section on the whole 220-mile circuit. Even Stonehaugh, the biggest settlement between Haltwhistle and Bellingham, is no more than a collection of forestry workers' houses round a village green, with no pub or shop. Your only chance of refreshments comes soon after leaving Haltwhistle, at the Twice Brewed Inn – so make sure you are carrying something to eat and drink.

If you have stayed overnight in Haltwhistle you need to retrace your route along Hadrian's Cycleway as far as Vindolanda, where Hadrian's Cycleway and the Pennine Cycleway split. You follow the Pennine Cycleway to Bellingham.

Shortly after crossing the B6318, 'Military Road' at Once Brewed, you have a fantastic view east towards Crag Lough and the cliffs along the line of Hadrian's Wall, leading towards Housesteads. If you are going to walk any part of Hadrian's Wall during the course of the ride, this is the best bit! Beyond the wall, the unfenced lane undulates over open rolling countryside past the last few outlying farms before Wark Forest. The tarmac ends at the point where a lane leads to Scotchcoulthard, with fine views ahead and a sign declaring it is 14 miles to Bellingham.

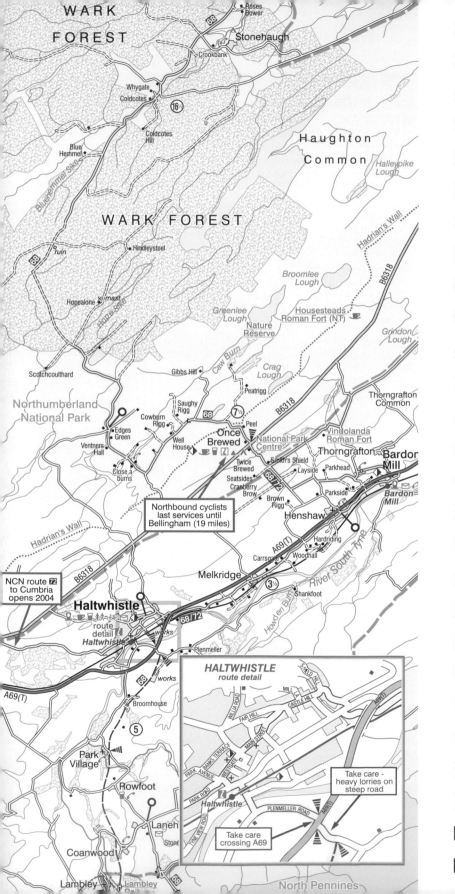

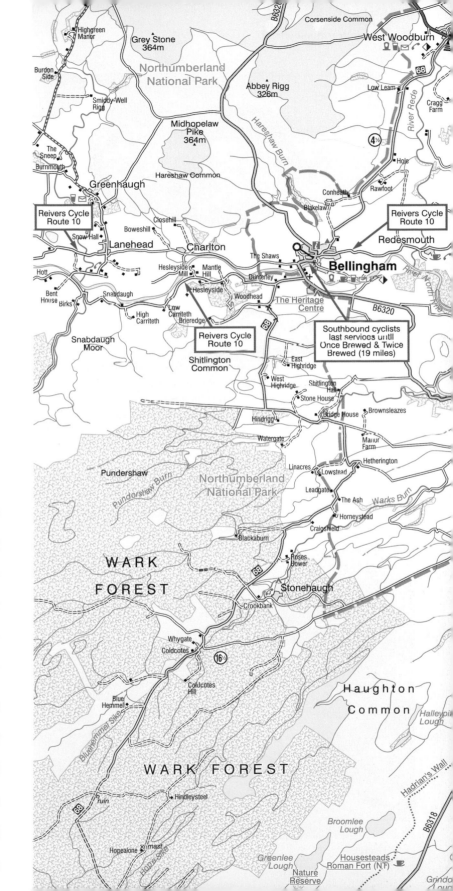

Cuddy's Crag, Hadrian's Wall

There are almost 5 miles on forest roads on the rollercoaster route through Wark Forest. Although passable by touring bike, you should go slowly down the descents, particularly if you are heavily laden, as Wark Forest is no place to break a pannier rack or bend a wheel. After rejoining tarmac you pass close to the small cluster of houses in the hamlet of Stonehaugh. Stonehaugh has no pub or store - you will need to push on to Bellingham to find these. A final 330ft (100m) climb after crossing the delightfully-named Houxty Burn takes you to the top of Ealinghamrigg Common, with splendid views north over the valley of the River North Tyne. As Bellingham (prounounced 'Bellinjum') is the largest settlement between Hexham and Rothbury, it punches above its weight with several shops, pubs, a cafe and fish and chip shop.

Bellingham

GRADE OF DIFFICULTY
Strenuous

MAJOR CLIMBS
1 460ft (140m) north from the valley of the South Tyne in Bardon Mill then after a brief downhill, a further 295ft (90m) beyond the Once Brewed Visitor Centre to Hound Hill, on the north side of Hadrian's Wall.
2 330ft (100m) along the unfenced road to the edge of Wark Forest.
3 Several short ups and downs through the forest.
4 330ft (100m) north from the crossing of Houxty Burn to the top of Ealinghamrigg Common before the final descent to Bellingham.

PUBLIC TRANSPORT
There are hourly trains between Newcastle and Haltwhistle throughout the week.

NATIONAL RAIL ENQUIRIES
08457 48 49 50

ARRIVA TRAINS NORTHERN
Customer Helpline
0870 602 3322
www.arrivatrainsnorthern.co.uk

Tyne Valley Coaches
runs a bus service from Hexham to Bellingham that carries bikes
01434 602217

TOURIST INFORMATION
HALTWHISTLE
01434 322002

ONCE BREWED (SEASONAL)
01434 344396

BELLINGHAM
01434 220616

BIKE SHOPS
HALTWHISTLE
THE BIKE SHOP
17 Westgate
01434 322544

EDEN'S LAWN SERVICE STATION
(cycle hire and spares only)
Bypass Road
01434 320443

BELLINGHAM
VILLAGE AND COUNTRY STORE
(limited spares only)
01434 220027

PLACES OF INTEREST
HALTWHISTLE
See page 25

VINDOLANDA
See page 25

ONCE BREWED
NORTHUMBERLAND NATIONAL PARK VISITOR CENTRE
01434 344396
There is a display of a history of the region since the retreat of the Ice Age glaciers. It stands on vallum - a broad earthwork that probably defined the military zone to the south of Hadrian's Wall.

BELLINGHAM
This small market town once had an iron industry that provided metalwork for the Tyne Bridge in Newcastle. The 12th-century Church of St Cuthbert has a roof made of stone slabs, which protected it against 16th-century marauders.

Bellingham from The Cheviot Hotel

REFRESHMENTS

With the exception of the pub and the (seasonal) visitor centre at Once Brewed, there is no refreshment at all between Haltwhistle and Bellingham. This is the most remote section of the whole route so plan accordingly. There are plenty of places to choose from in Haltwhistle and Bellingham.

At Once Brewed, there is the Twice Brewed Inn, and cafe at the visitor centre.

ACCOMMODATION

BARDON MILL & ONCE BREWED

ONCE BREWED YOUTH HOSTEL
Military Road
01434 344360
email: oncebrewed@yha.org.uk

MONTCOFFER
01434 344138
www.montcoffer.co.uk

TWICE BREWED INN
Military Road
01434 344534
www.twicebrewedinn.co.uk

CRAWS NEST
East Twice Brewed Farm
01434 344348

VALLUM LODGE
Military Road, Twice Brewed
01434 344488
www.vallum-lodge.co.uk

BELLINGHAM

YHA BELLINGHAM,
Woodburn Road
www.yha.org.uk
0870 770 5694

THE CHEVIOT HOTEL
Main Street
01434 220696
www.thecheviothotel.co.uk

LYNDALE GUEST HOUSE
Off the Square
01434 220321
www.lyndaleguesthouse.co.uk

LYNN VIEW
01434 220344

WESTFIELD HOUSE
01434 220340

Bellingham to Alwinton/Rothbury

22 miles, road route (signed) Moderate
40 miles, forest route (unsigned) Strenuous
Follow Pennine Cycleway, Route 68

There are two options for this stage north from Bellingham. One takes
you up the valley of the River Rede (a tributary of the Tyne) and through
Elsdon and Harbottle to Alwinton. The other – a route not always open
(see below) – uses forest roads through Redesdale Forest, then climbs on
a military road past Cottonshopehead to a spectacular high point of
1,670ft (510m) in the heart of the Cheviots before dropping down to
Alwinton, along the valley of the River Coquet. The forest route option
crosses military ranges, and the access road is closed to the public when
firing is taking place. Telephone the Range Liaison Officer (0191 261 1046)
to check opening times before taking this route option from Bellingham.

Road route via Elsdon

For a route that ostensibly follows a river valley (that of the River Rede),
the section from Bellingham to the A696 is anything but flat. But the two
main climbs, one either side of the A68, do give you sweeping views over
this lovely and remote countryside. A newly-built cyclepath along the
A696 saves you from this fast road. If the cyclists' cafe in Elsdon, just off
the vast village green, is open it is well worth a visit. Its walls are
festooned with pictures of racing cyclists, the teapots are bottomless and

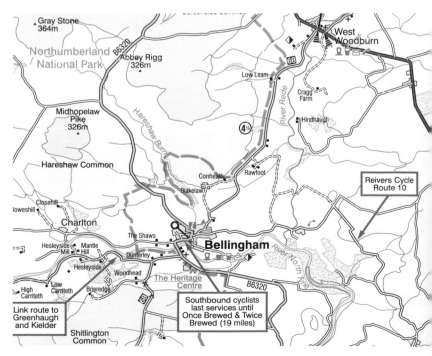

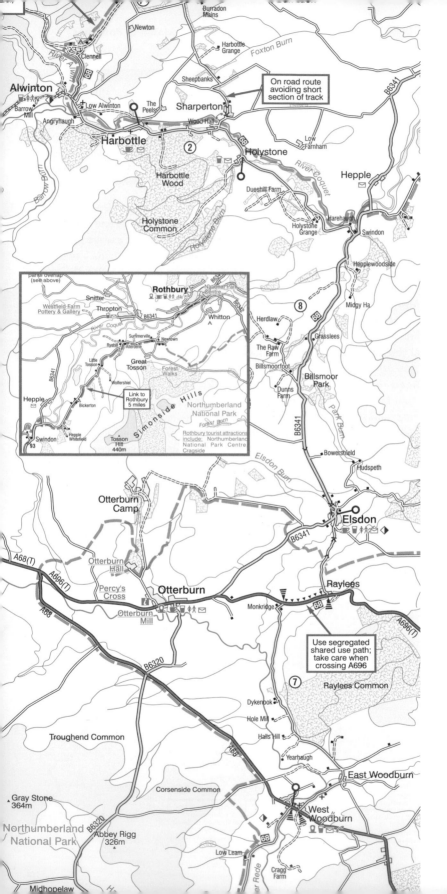

the cakes are specially prepared to maximise the energy they give you! You will certainly need a good pair of legs to take you to the top of the hill that follows the crossing of Elsdon Burn. The climb is, as ever, rewarded with wide-ranging views, particularly north-east down Coquetdale to the hills above Rothbury, rising to over 1,000ft (305m). This is the last big climb of the day, but there are still several smaller ones along the valley of the River Coquet as you pass through the attractive stone-built villages of Holystone and Harbottle to Alwinton, all three settlements boasting handsome churches and pubs. Alternatively, if you choose to stay in Rothbury, you follow Coquetdale eastwards on a minor road on the south side of the valley.

Rothbury High Street

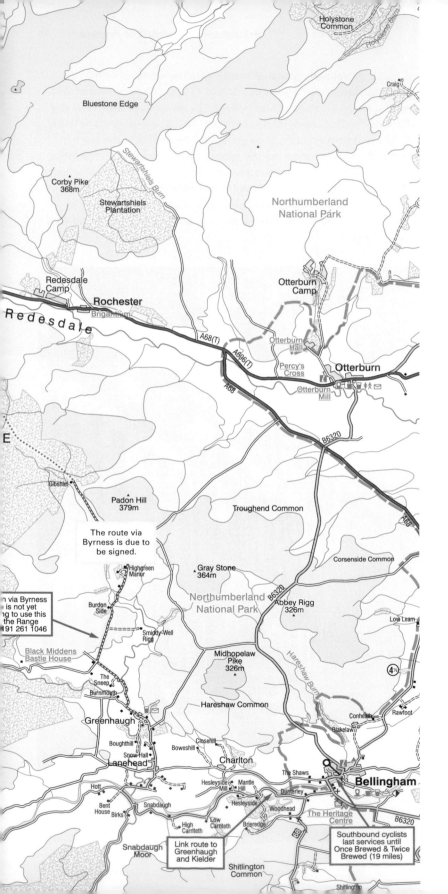

Off-road route via Redesdale Forest and the military road

This spectacular ride is only open at certain times, and you need to check with the Army (see page 33) before undertaking the stretch from the A68 near Byrness to the Chew Green Roman camps at the top of Upper Coquetdale. Mountain bikes are recommended for this forest option.

Oddly enough, you head south from Bellingham to start, as the lane on the south side of the Tyne valley is much quieter than that on the north side. You pass a lovely line of beech and sycamore trees, through a landscape of pasture and woodland bounded by neat stone walls, with views to the hills to the north of the Tyne. Stone-built farms and barns are evenly spaced along the valley, through Lanehead to Greenhaugh. With its few cottages, pub and school, Greenhaugh is the largest settlement on this off-road alternative for the next 30 miles, until Alwinton, way down the Coquet valley.

The tarmac ends about 5 miles after Greenhaugh, on the edge of the forest, towards the end of a long steady climb of almost 650ft (200m) from Greenhaugh up to the high point in the forest. At the summit, the Pennine Cycleway joins the Pennine Way long-distance footpath, on its way from Edale in the Peak District to Kirk Yetholm in the Scottish Borders. The route is shared by both trails along the forest road on a second, shorter climb then a long fast descent down to the information board by the bridge over the River Rede at Blakehopeburnhaugh.

Rough pastureland above Elsdon

A slightly circuitous route through the forest and past the caravan site at Cottonshopeburnfoot minimises time spent on the busy A68, dropping you close to the start of the military road that follows the valley of the Cottonshope Burn. This is the section that is sometimes closed for firing practice. The road climbs higher and higher, up above the tree line to a bleak moorland summit with enormous views in all directions. The summit represents the point where you cross watersheds – from that of the Tyne, which you have been following since Newcastle, to that of the River Coquet, which flows east to reach the North Sea at Amble. In the next 13 miles you drop 1,150 feet (350m) alongside an ever growing River Coquet. Be warned that there are a couple of short climbs along the course of this section. After so long in the wilderness, are you ready for the bright lights of Alwinton?

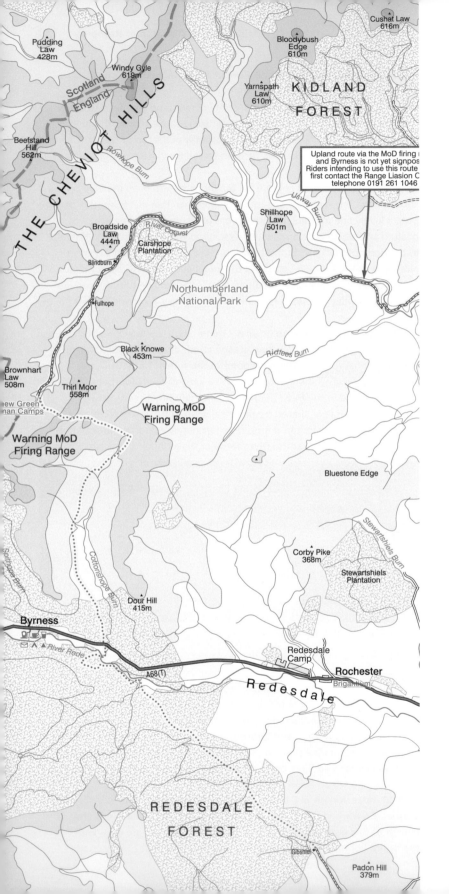

Pudding
Law
428m

Windy Gyle
619m

Scotland

England

THE CHEVIOT HILLS

Beefstand
Hill
562m

Rowhope Burn

Bloodybush
Edge
610m

Cushat Law
616m

Yarnspath
Law
610m

KIDLAND

FOREST

Usway Burn

Upland route via the MoD firing
and Byrness is not yet signpos
Riders intending to use this route
first contact the Range Liasion C
telephone 0191 261 1046

Broadside
Law
444m

River Coquet

Carshope
Plantation

Blindburn

Shillhope
Law
501m

Fulhope

Northumberland
National Park

Black Knowe
453m

Ridlees Burn

Brownhart
Law
508m

Thirl Moor
558m

ew Green
nan Camps

Warning MoD
Firing Range

Bluestone Edge

Warning MoD
Firing Range

Spithope Burn

Cottonshope Burn

Corby Pike
368m

Stewartshiels Burn

Stewartshiels
Plantation

Dour Hill
415m

Byrness

River Rede

A68(T)

Redesdale
Camp

Rochester

Brigantium

R e d e s d a l e

REDESDALE

FOREST

Gibshiel

Padon Hill
379m

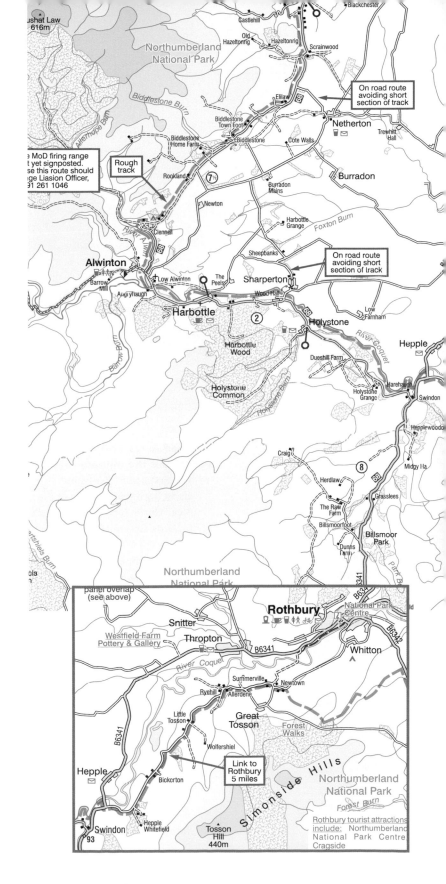

On road route avoiding short section of track

Rough track

e MoD firing range
t yet signposted.
se this route should
ge Liasion Officer,
91 261 1046

On road route avoiding short section of track

Northumberland National Park

Biddlestone Burn

Blackchester

Castlehill

Old Hazeltonrig   Hazeltonrig

Scrainwood

Elilaw

Netherton

Trewhitt Hall

Cote Walls

Burradon

Biddlestone Town Foot

Biddlestone

Biddlestone Home Farm

Rookland

7½

Newton

Burradon Mains

Harbottle Grange

Foxton Burn

Clennell

Sheepbanks

Alwinton

Barrow Mill

Low Alwinton

The Peels

Sharperton

Wood Hall

Low Farnham

Angryhaugh

Harbottle

2

Holystone

Hepple

River Coquet

Harbottle Wood

Dueshill Farm

Harehaugh

Holystone Grange

Swindon

Holystone Common

Holystone Burn

Hepplewoodo

Craig

8

Midgy Ha

Herdlaw

The Raw Farm

Grasslees

Billsmoorfoot

Billsmoor Park

Dunns Farm

Northumberland National Park

panel overlap (see above)

Rothbury

National Park Centre

Snitter

Thropton

Westfield Farm Pottery & Gallery

B6341

Whitton

River Coquet

Summerville   Newtown

Ryehill   Allerdene

Little Tosson

Great Tosson

Forest Walks

Wolfershiel

Link to Rothbury 5 miles

Hepple

Bickerton

Simonside Hills

Northumberland National Park

Forest Burn

Swindon

93

Hepple Whitefield

Tosson Hill 440m

Rothbury tourist attractions include: Northumberland National Park Centre Cragside

Fine tracks through Redesdale Forest

GRADE OF DIFFICULTY
Road route – moderate
Off-road route – strenuous

MAJOR CLIMBS
Road route via Elsdon
1   230ft (70m) climb northeast from Bellingham to Raw Side.
2   200ft (60m) north of East Woodburn.
3   230ft (70m) from crossing Raylees Burn to Gallow Hill south of Elsdon.
4   360ft (110m) north of Elsdon along the B6341.
5   (Rothbury option only)165ft (50m) on the minor lane link to the main route.

Off-road route via Redesdale Forest and the military road
1   The first 215ft (65m) climb starts from the crossing of the River North Tyne and continues towards Greenhaugh.
2   Before the forest there is a 460ft (140m) climb from crossing the stream beyond Greenhaugh to the T-junction by Pit Houses.
3   Two climbs of 265ft (80m) and 165ft (50m) through the forest.
4   The biggest hill on the whole 220-mile circuit climbs 985ft (300m) from the A68 north along the military road to the summit above Chew Green Roman Camps.
5   The road drops 1,150ft (350m) down to Alwinton (hurrah!) but be warned - there are still a couple of unexpected small climbs during the course of the descent.

Handsome Coquetdale Farmhouse

PUBLIC TRANSPORT

There is a bus service that carries bikes between Hexham and Bellingham. See page 30.

TOURIST INFORMATION

BELLINGHAM
01434 220616

OTTERBURN
01830 520093

ROTHBURY (SEASONAL)
01669 620887

BIKE SHOPS

BELLINGHAM

VILLAGE AND COUNTRY STORE
(limited spares only)
01434 220027

ROTHBURY

SPAR SUPERMARKET
(Cycle hire only)
Main Street
01669 621338/620360

PLACES OF INTEREST

BELLINGHAM
See page 31

ELSDON
The village is scattered around a large green with a peel tower and the earthworks of a Norman castle. In 1877, three horse skulls were found in the belfry of the 14th-century church - they were said to protect the building from lightning. More important from a cyclist's viewpoint is the cyclists' cafe just off the green.

HOLYSTONE
A footpath leads from the village to Lady's Well, where, in the 7th century, St Paulinus is said to have baptised 3,000 Celtic converts in one day.

ROTHBURY
An elegant market town set on the steep bank of the River Coquet. Just to the east of town is Cragside

House (01669 620633/620150), built in Victorian times by the industrialist, Sir William Armstrong, and probably the first house to be lit by electricity. The house and grounds are open to the public.

Off-road route via Redesdale Forest and the military road

Chew Green Roman Camp
This is the site of three earthwork camps and a small permanent fortlet; the earliest camp dates from AD80 when Agricola, Governor of Britain, was subjugating fierce local tribes.

REFRESHMENTS

There are plenty of places to choose from in Bellingham. In smaller villages, try the following:

West Woodburn – Bay Horse Inn, shop

Elsdon – Bird in Bush pub, Cyclists' cafe

Harbottle – Star pub, Coquet Crafts tea room

Alwinton – Rose & Thistle pub

Off-road route via Byrness
Greenhaugh – Hollybush Inn

Byrness – Hotel (bar and food)

ACCOMMODATION

Youth Hostel (for western, off-road option via Redesdale Forest:

YHA BYRNESS
7 Otterburn Green
Byrness
0870 770 5740
email: reservations@yha.org.uk

GREENHAUGH
Northwest of Bellingham on the western, forest alternative

HOLLYBUSH INN
01434 240391
www.vizual4U.co.uk/hollybush

HARBOTTLE

THE BYRE
01669 650476
email: rosemary@the-byre.co.uk

ALWINTON

ROSE & THISTLE
01669 650226
email:
enqs@roseandthistlealwinton
.com

COQUETDALE B&B
2 Gallowlaw
01669 650253
dagg@alwinton.fsbusiness.co.uk

NEWTON FARM COTTAGES
Newton near Alwinton
01669 650490

ROTHBURY

THE QUEENS HEAD
Townfoot
01669 620740
www.queensheadrothbury.com

SILVERTON LODGE
Silverton Lane
01669 620144
www.silvertonlodge.co.uk

KATERINA'S GUEST HOUSE
Cathryn Mills, High Street
01669 620691
www.katerinasguesthouse.co.uk

THE HAVEN
Back Crofts
01669 620577
www.thehavenrothbury.co.uk

ORCHARD GUEST HOUSE
High Street
01669 620684
email:
jpickard@orchardguesthouse.co.uk

Alwinton or Rothbury to Wooler

23 miles
Moderate/Strenuous
Follow Pennine Cycleway, Route 68

Foothills of the Cheviots above Ingram

This lovely stage runs along the eastern fringe of the Northumberland National Park, neatly avoiding the need to use or cross the busy A697 by linking networks of quiet lanes, bridleways, byways and footbridges over rivers and streams. The countryside is so quiet and unchanged that at times it seems you are in a parallel world, far away from the 21st century.

From the start in Alwinton, the ride follows an open unfenced lane alongside the pretty River Alwin, soon passing between the pillars of Clennell Hall and through the caravan site. You climb on a rough track through woodland to emerge in an open field with fine views – but plenty of gates. If you prefer to avoid this short off-road section, there is a perfectly good lane alternative that runs parallel to the waymarked route.

Beyond Alnham, the Pennine Cycleway map shows three options for continuing northwards. The westernmost route, over Wether Hill, is very rough and should only be undertaken on mountain bikes, preferably lightly laden and after a period of several dry days, as the southern part is liable to get very muddy. Of the two other routes, the middle one via Mile End Farm is shorter by about four miles and involves less climbing. The easternmost route takes you past the lovely parkland surrounding Eslington Park, and gives you the chance of refreshment in the cafes and pubs in Glanton and Powburn. The two road routes link in Branton and cross the River Breamish via a new footbridge (replacing the one that washed away in floods in 2001). The Breamish is one of several rivers that

Rolling countryside above Glanton

rise on the Cheviots and flow north to join the River Till, which in turn joins the mighty River Tweed to the north-west of Coldstream.

It is well worth a short detour to the Northumberland National Park Visitor Centre at Ingram, with its displays of local history and wildlife. The Cheviot Hills are constant companions on this stretch of the ride, although the highest peak, The Cheviot (2,675ft / 815m), is frequently in cloud.

After a steady climb north from Ingram you have two short, scenic off-road sections. The first is an amazing dingly-dell descent to a small footbridge over the River Roddam. You will certainly have to walk some of this. The second (longer) section takes you through some fine parkland with recently-planted hedgerows and trees and beautiful rolling countryside, only slightly marred by the obtrusive line of pylons between Newcastle and Coldstream.

Views start opening up of the hills on the other side of the valley formed by the River Till, the last range of hills before the North Sea coast. A final ford / footbridge and a final climb set you up for a wonderful descent into Wooler, the largest town between Alnwick and Berwick, with plenty of places to stay and eat.

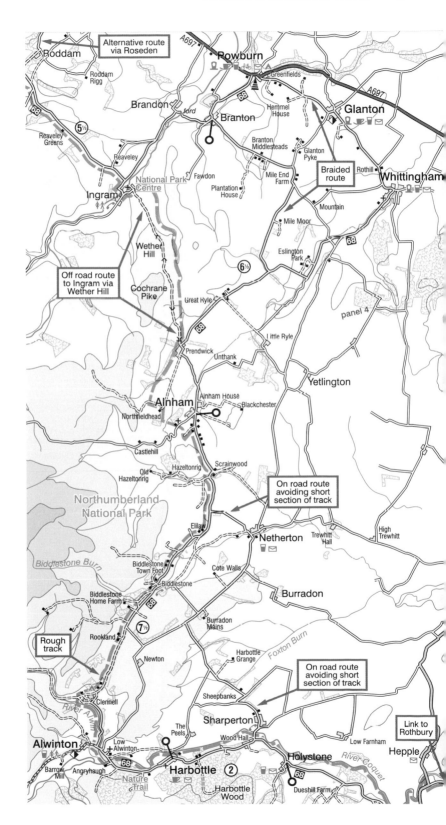

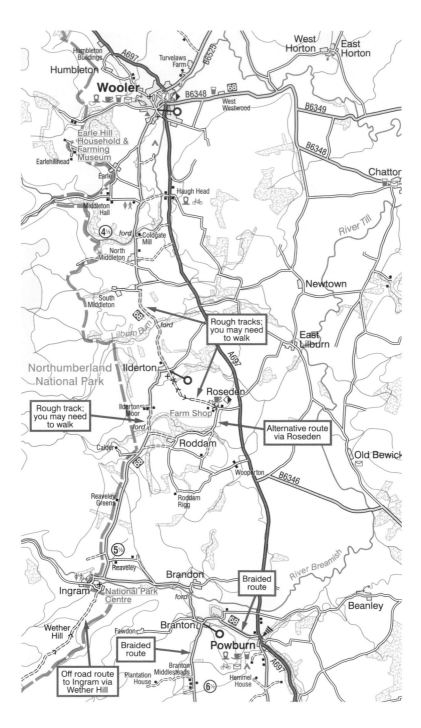

North of Ilderton

GRADE OF DIFFICULTY

Moderate / strenuous

MAJOR CLIMBS

1 Starting from Alwinton, there is a 330ft (100m) climb on the track northeast from Clennell.

2 The second 200ft (60m) climb tackles the foothills of the Cheviots between Alnham and Great Ryle.

3 The third 330ft (100m) climb takes you out of the valley of the River Breamish north towards Ilderton.

4 There are several short (but at times steep) climbs on the off-road sections to Wooler.

PUBLIC TRANSPORT

None nearby. A possible (long) day ride would be to follow the Pennine Cycleway between Berwick and Whittingham (south of Wooler), then cut across country on quiet roads via Shilbottle to Alnmouth (OS Landranger map 81), using the train service between Alnmouth and Berwick to complete the loop. This could be done in either direction depending on wind direction and train times.

TOURIST INFORMATION

ROTHBURY (SEASONAL)

01669 620887

WOOLER (SEASONAL)

01668 282123

BIKE SHOPS

ROTHBURY

SPAR SUPERMARKET

(Hire and spares only)
Main Street 01669 621338

WOOLER

FERGUSONS MOTORS AND CYCLES

(Cycle hire)
Haugh Head Garage
South Road
01668 281316 / 281687

PLACES OF INTEREST

WOOLER

Wooler suffered a major fire in 1862 and most of the houses in the town were built after that date. It is the largest town between Berwick and Alnwick and a centre for fishing and hiking in the Cheviot Hills. There are many pubs and cafes and a wide variety of shops. Near the market place is the mound of a Norman castle which guarded the highway to the south. Earle Hill Museum (01668 281243) contains old domestic and farming equipment. The Cheviot Centre (01668 282406) houses Wooler Tourist Information Centre and has information about local landscapes, wildlife and walks.

REFRESHMENTS

There are plenty of places to choose from in Rothbury and Wooler.

In smaller villages, try:

Alwinton – Rose & Thistle pub

Rothbury – lots of choice

Glanton – Queens Head pub, cafe and shop

Powburn – Plough pub, Poachers Rest cafe (on the main road north of the village)

Quiet lanes south of Wooler

ACCOMMODATION

POWBURN

LOW HEDGELEY FARM
01665 578815

CRAWLEY FARMHOUSE
01665 578413

WOOLER

WOOLER YOUTH HOSTEL
30 Cheviot Street,
Wooler NE71 6LW
0870 770 6100

BLACK BULL HOTEL
2 High Street
01668 281309
www.theblackbullhotel.co.uk

TANKERVILLE ARMS HOTEL
22 Cottage Road
01668 281581
www.tankervillehotel.co.uk

RYECROFT HOTEL
28 Ryecroft Way
01668 281459
www.ryecroft-hotel.com

TILLDALE HOUSE
34/40 High Street
01668 281450

WINTON HOUSE
39 Glendale Road
01668 281362
www.wintonhouse.ntb.org.uk

ST HILLIERS
6 Church Street
01668 281340

WEST WEETWOOD FARM
B6348, east of Wooler
01668 281497

Wooler to Berwick-upon-Tweed

28 miles
Easy/Moderate
Follow Pennine Cycleway, Route 68
and Coast and Castles, Route 1

This is one of the easiest sections on the whole circuit, all on tarmac and well surfaced paths with few climbs. Crossing undulating countryside of arable fields with huge skies and big open spaces, this is a landscape that can be found all the way up the east coast of Britain from East Anglia to Aberdeenshire.

The ride leaves Wooler and largely follows the broad valley of the River Till north towards the Scottish border. Two beautiful, traffic-free sections between Wooler and Doddington and between Heatherslaw and Etal have recently opened. Several highlights along the way may tempt you to dismount and enjoy a bit of culture with a teashop / cafe / pub thrown in. The first is the model village of Ford, with its castle and fine buildings including art and craft exhibitions. Just down the road is Heatherslaw Mill, a working water mill powered by the River Till, with a good cafe selling cakes made from Heatherslaw flour. Etal also has a castle and a thatched pub, the Black Bull, that would not look out of place in a Devon village.

A third castle lies just on the exit of Norham, an attractive village with a wide main street, situated right on the border with Scotland. It is in Norham that the Pennine Cycleway, Route 68 joins Route 1 on its long and winding course from the Shetlands to Dover. It is one of those wonderful quirks of the National Cycle Network that as you are heading north on Route 68 into Berwick you are also heading south on Route 1. Work that one out! The two routes share the same course as far as Berwick-upon-Tweed, the end point for the Pennine Cycleway but about two thirds of the way around the Northumbria's Cycle Kingdom circuit (if you have started from Newcastle).

The Chain Bridge Honey Farm (open Easter to the end of October) lies at the top of the hill that takes you down across the Union Suspension Bridge and into Scotland. Your time in Scotland is likely to be brief, as the route is only across the border for three miles, running alongside the peculiarly eroded pink sandstone wall around Paxton House then passing the lions on the pillars at the entrance to the house itself. The route crosses back into England to arrive at the amazing walled ramparts of Berwick-upon-Tweed. As you approach Berwick there are great views of the mighty railway viaduct spanning the River Tweed as it reaches its journey's end at the North Sea.

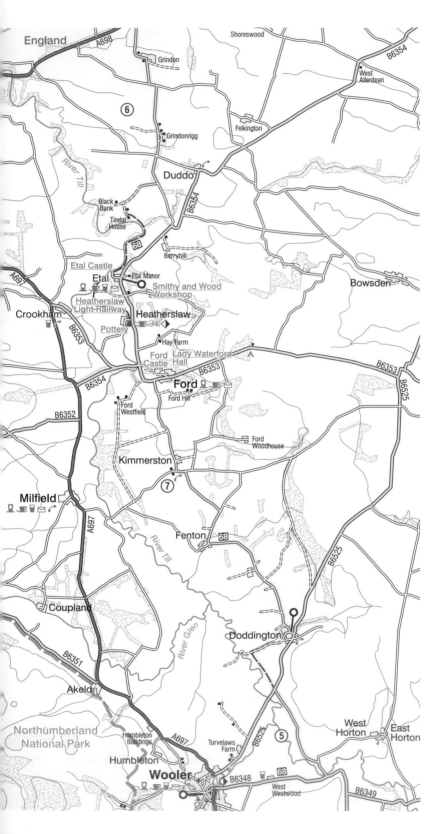

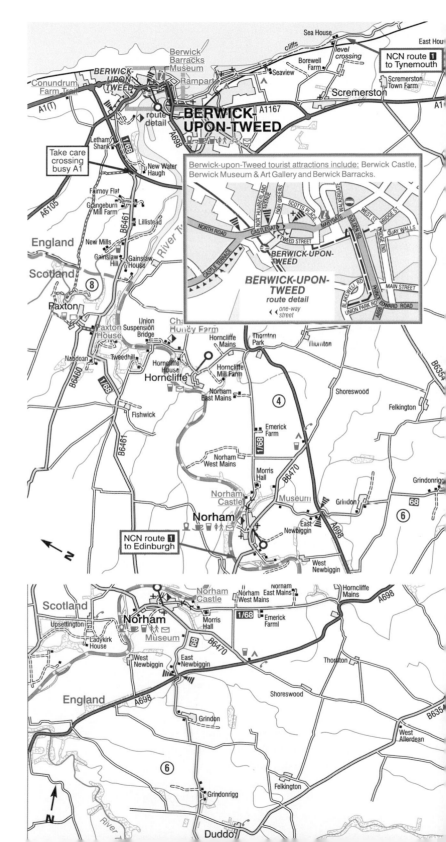

Berwick-upon-Tweed tourist attractions include: Berwick Castle, Berwick Museum & Art Gallery and Berwick Barracks.

BERWICK-UPON-TWEED
route detail

‹‹ one-way street

Railway viaduct spanning the River Tweed

GRADE OF DIFFICULTY
Easy / moderate

MAJOR CLIMBS
A day of undulating countryside
with no climb more than 120ft (35m)

PUBLIC TRANSPORT
There is a regular fast train service
between Edinburgh and Newcastle
that stops at Berwick. A possible
55-mile day ride would be to follow
the Pennine Cycleway between
Berwick and Whittingham (south of
Wooler) then cut across country on
quiet roads via Shilbottle to
Alnmouth (OS Landranger map 81),
using the train service between
Alnmouth and Berwick to complete
the loop. This could be done in
either direction depending on wind
direction and convenient train
times. A free map, Northumbria's
Cycling Kingdom, showing this
route option (although at a less
detailed scale than the OS map) is
available from Sustrans.

TOURIST INFORMATION

WOOLER (SEASONAL)
01668 282123

BERWICK UPON TWEED
01289 330733

BIKE SHOPS

WOOLER

FERGUSONS MOTORS AND CYCLES
(Also cycle hire)
Haugh Head Garage
South Road
01668 281316/281687

HEATHERSLAW MILL
(Cycle hire only)
01890 820338 or 820664

BERWICK

TWEED CYCLES
(Also cycle hire)
17a Bridge Street
01289 331476

HALFORDS
Northumberland Road
Tweedmouth
01289 330771

PLACES OF INTEREST

WOOLER
See page 47

DODDINGTON
The village is grouped around the ruins of the 1584 peel tower. The church has a watch house built in 1826 to guard against body snatchers.

Ford Castle

HEATHERSLAW
Visit the working mill and museum of milling machinery with an attached cafe. The railway museum has photographs, relics and exhibits. 01890 820338

ETAL
The village consists of a single street of whitewashed houses, some of which are thatched, leading to the ruined gatehouse of the 14th-century castle (01890 820332). Below, on the River Till, is a weir where salmon leap.

NORHAM
Towering over the the village on a loop of the River Tweed is the 90ft wall of the ruined Norman keep (01890 382329). The Station Museum recalls the Kelso branch line, the oldest in the county, with the original signal box, booking office and porter's room (01289 382217).

UNION CHAIN BRIDGE
Linking Scotland to England across the River Tweed, the bridge was built in 1829 by Samuel Brown and was the first of its kind in Britain. The Chain Bridge Honey Farm is worth a visit (01289 386362)

BERWICK-UPON-TWEED
England's northernmost town has elegant Georgian streets and a square dominated by the spire of the 18th-century town hall. Whether you are staying or just passing through it is well worth doing the 2-mile walk around the Elizabethan walls encircling the town. The Georgian barracks contain an exhibition of the history of the British infantry. Three bridges span the River Tweed: the 15-arch Jacobean stone bridge, Robert Stephenson's 1847 railway bridge and the A1 road bridge of 1928.

REFRESHMENTS
There are plenty of places to choose from in Wooler and Berwick.

In smaller villages, try:
Ford – teas at Post Office
Heatherslaw Mill – tearoom
Etal – Black Bull pub, tearoom at shop

Norham – Victoria Hotel, Masons Arms
Horncliffe – Fishers Arms pub and
Chain Bridge Honey Farm (open Easter to end of October)
Paxton (just off the route) - The Cross Inn

Union Bridge between Horncliffe and Paxton

ACCOMMODATION

FORD

THE ESTATE HOUSE
01890 820668

THE OLD POST OFFICE
2 Old Post Office Cottages
01890 820286
www.secretkingdom.com

NORHAM

DROMORE HOUSE
12 Pedwell Way
01289 382313

ROSEMARY COTTAGE
14 West Street
01289 552544

BERWICK UPON TWEED

BERWICK BACKPACKERS
56 Bridge Street
01289 331481
www.bkbackpacker.co.uk

THE OLD VICARAGE
Church Road
Tweedmouth
01289 306909
www.oldvicarageberwick.co.uk

CARA HOUSE
44 Castlegate
01289 302749
email: pam@carahouse.plus.com

EASTFIELD HOUSE
6 North Road
01289 308949
www.eastfieldhouse-berwick.co.uk

RAVENSHOLME HOTEL
34-36 Ravensdowne
01289 308869

DERVAIG GUEST HOUSE
1 North Road
01289 307378
www.dervaig-guesthouse.co.uk

BRIDGE VIEW
14 Tweed Street
01289 308098

COBBLED YARD HOTEL
40 Walkergate
01289 308407
www.cobbleyardhotel.com

ROB ROY
Dock Road
Tweedmouth
01289 306428
www.therobroy.co.uk

Berwick-upon-Tweed to Bamburgh

23 miles
Easy/Moderate
Follow Coast and Castles Cycle Route 1

This part of the ride, along with the next, are the two most spectacular coastal days of the whole 220-mile circuit, with long, unbroken sections along the beautiful Northumbrian Coast, using tracks (at times rough) and quiet roads. You can also take a short detour to Holy Island (Lindisfarne). This stage finishes at Bamburgh, arguably the most impressive of all the castles along the coast.

If you spent the night in Berwick but were too tired to walk the town walls, try to do it before you leave! It is a splendid, airy stroll around the grassy ramparts, with wonderful views out to sea and back across the town's old buildings.

Leaving Berwick via back streets close to the docks and industrial area, south of the town, a short climb takes you to the end of the tarmac and up on to the cliffs, overlooking the North Sea. There are fantastic views ahead, although the track can be rough and muddy (as well as passing through fields grazed by livestock). By the end of 2005, through negotiations with landowners, a new course for the route should keep you on the east side of the main rail line between Goswick / Beachcomber House and the causeway to the Holy Island of Lindisfarne.

River Tweed Railway Viaduct

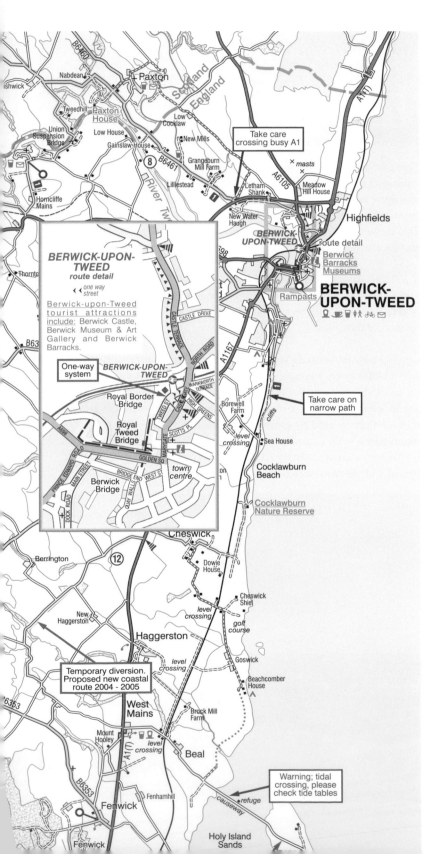

BERWICK-UPON-TWEED

BERWICK-UPON-TWEED
route detail

‹‹ *one way street*

Berwick-upon-Tweed tourist attractions include: Berwick Castle, Berwick Museum & Art Gallery and Berwick Barracks.

One-way system

BERWICK-UPON-TWEED

Royal Border Bridge

Royal Tweed Bridge

Berwick Bridge

town centre

Take care crossing busy A1

Take care on narrow path

Temporary diversion. Proposed new coastal route 2004 - 2005

Warning; tidal crossing, please check tide tables

Berwick Barracks Museums

Ramparts

BERWICK-UPON-TWEED

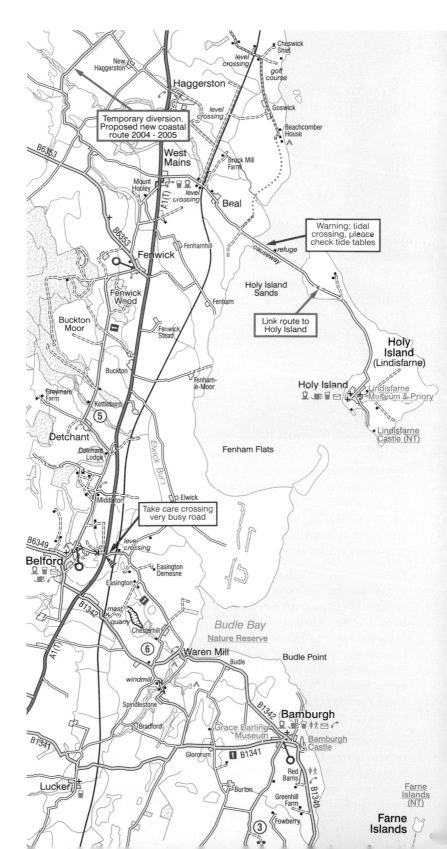

Temporary diversion.
Proposed new coastal
route 2004 - 2005

Warning; tidal
crossing, please
check tide tables

Link route to
Holy Island

Take care crossing
very busy road

Cheswick
Shiel

level
crossing

golf
course

New
Haggerston

level
crossing

Haggerston

Goswick

level
crossing

Beachcomber
House

West
Mains

Brock Mill
Farm

B6353

Mount
Hooley

A1(T)

level
crossing

Beal

B6353

Fenhamhill

causeway   refuge

Fenwick

Holy Island
Sands

Fenwick
Wood

Fenham

Buckton
Moor

Fenwick
Stead

Holy
Island
(Lindisfarne)

Buckton

Fenham-
le-Moor

Holy Island

Lindisfarne
Museum & Priory

Greymare
Farm

Kettleburn

⑤

Lindisfarne
Castle (NT)

Detchant

Detchant
Lodge

Fenham Flats

Elwick Burn

Middleton

Elwick

B6349

level
crossing

Belford

Easington
Demesne

Easington

B1342

mast
quarry

Chesterhill

Budle Bay
Nature Reserve

⑥

Waren Mill

Budle

Budle Point

A1(T)

windmill

Spindlestone

B1342

Bamburgh

Bradford

Grace Darling
Museum

Bamburgh
Castle

B1341

Glororum

B1341

Red
Barns

Lucker

Burton

Greenhill
Farm

B1340

Farne
Islands
(NT)

③

Fowberry

Farne
Islands

Bamburgh Castle

Farm cottages near Cheswick

A side trip to Lindisfarne's castle and priory is thoroughly worthwhile, although you need to check tide times, as the causeway is flooded at high tide (see www.northumberland.gov.uk/vg/holyisland or telephone Berwick TIC 01289 330 733). The island has several pubs, cafes and tearooms – the one drawback could be battling back to the mainland in the teeth of the prevailing westerly wind.

The countryside unfolds as arable fields and pasture, bounded by scraggy hedgerows or stone walls, with big, solid, stone-built farmhouses along the way. The relatively flat topography gives the illusion of huge skies, pierced by the outline of the Cheviots to the south-west. The first noticeable hill after Berwick comes on the approach to Belford, marking the start of a range of hills between the Cheviots and the coast. Stretching from near Belford in the north to Rothbury and Morpeth in the south, they rise to between 600 and 900ft (185 and 275m), plunging twice for the Rivers Aln and Coquet. The Coast & Castles Route largely skirts these hills to the east, staying close to the coast.

South-east from Belford towards Bamburgh, a delightful wooded lane passes the round tower of an old windmill and swoops to cross Waren Burn. You join the B1341 west of Glororum for a long gentle descent, with the splendid sight of Bamburgh Castle set against the backdrop of the Farne Islands.

GRADE OF DIFFICULTY

Easy / moderate
Some sections have rough
surfaces, which are harder.

MAJOR CLIMBS

1 Although there are no big
   climbs between Berwick and
   the crossing of the A1 at West
   Mains, there are some rough
   surfaces where even the
   gentlest gradient can make it
   hard going.
2 There is a steady climb of 280ft
   (85m) from near the A1 at West
   Mains to Belford.

PUBLIC TRANSPORT

Virgin and GNER operate train
services between Newcastle,
Alnmouth and Berwick. National
Rail enquiries 08457 484950

What about a day ride?

Several trains a day go from Alnmouth to Berwick and Newcastle,
departing approximately every 1½
to 2 hrs from 0800 - 2000 hrs
Monday to Friday, with a
considerably reduced service at the
weekends. It would be feasible to
cycle one way between Alnmouth
and Berwick as a day ride, letting
the train take the strain for the
other half of the journey. Check to
see which way the wind is blowing
(you want it on your back when
you are cycling) before deciding
which way to pedal.

TOURIST INFORMATION

BERWICK UPON TWEED
01289 330733

SEAHOUSES (SEASONAL)
01665 720884

ADDERSTONE, NEAR BELFORD
01668 213678

BIKE SHOPS

BERWICK UPON TWEED

HALFORDS
Northumberland Road
Tweedmouth
01289 330771

TWEED CYCLES
(Also cycle hire)
17a Bridge Street
01289 331476

PLACES OF INTEREST

BERWICK UPON TWEED
SEE PAGE 53

HOLY ISLAND OF LINDISFARNE
Incoming tides cut off this ancient
monastic site, now a paradise for
birdwatchers. The romantic castle
perched on the cone of rock was a
ruin until it was rebuilt in 1903. A
monastery was founded by St
Aidan in AD634 then destroyed by
the Vikings. This was replaced in
1093 by the priory, now a roofless
ruin. The illuminated 7th-century
Lindisfarne Gospels are located in
the British Museum.

BAMBURGH
The village's pretty 18th-century
cottages are dwarfed by the 12th-
century castle, perched on a 150ft
coastal crag. Battlements provide
views to the Cheviot Hills in the
west and the Farne Islands in the
east. There is a museum (01668
214465) devoted to the lighthouse
keeper's daughter, Grace Darling,
who rowed out with her father to
rescue shipwreck survivors in 1838.

REFRESHMENTS

There are plenty of places to choose from in Berwick upon Tweed.

In smaller villages, try:

Scremerston – (just off route) Cafe and farm shop at Pot a Doodle Do Arts Centre, Borewell Farm

West Mains (A1) – Plough Hotel, shop at garage

Belford – Blue Bell Hotel, Black Swan pub, several stores

Bamburgh – Lord Crewe Arms pub, Victoria Hotel, Copper Kettle tearooms, shops

ACCOMMODATION

BEAL (WEST OF HOLY ISLAND)

WEST MAINS HOUSE
01289 381227

BROCKMILL FARMHOUSE
01289 381283
www.lindisfarne.org.uk/brock-mill-farmhouse

HOLY ISLAND

CROWN & ANCHOR HOTEL
Market Place
01289 389215
www.crownandanchorinn.co.uk

LINDISFARNE HOTEL
01289 389273

THE SHIP INN
Marygate
01289 389311

NORTH VIEW LODGE
Marygate
01289 389222

BRITANNIA HOUSE
01289 389218

THE BUNGALOW
Chare Ends
01289 389308

BELFORD

THE FARMHOUSE GUESTHOUSE
24 West Street
01668 213083
email: famhouseguesthouse@tiscali.co.uk

MARKET CROSS
1 Church Street
01668 213013
www.marketcross.net

BLUE BELL FARM HOUSE
West Street
01668 213890

BAMBURGH

GLENANDER
27 Lucker Road
01668 214336
wwww.glenander.com

BROOME
22 Ingram Road
01668 214 287
www.member.xoom.com/bamburgh

GREENGATES
Front Street
01668 214535
www.greengatesbamburgh.co.uk

HILLCREST HOUSE
29 Lucker Road
01668 214639
www.hillcrest-bamburgh.co.uk

HILLSIDE
25 Lucker Road
01668 214674
www.hillside-bamburgh.com

SQUIRREL COTTAGE
1, Friar's Court
01668 214494

THE MIZEN HEAD HOTEL
Lucker Road
01668 214254

THE SUNNINGDALE HOTEL
21-23 Lucker Road
01668 214334
www.sunningdale-hotel.com

Bamburgh to Amble

28 miles
Moderate
Follow Coast and Castles Cycle Route 1

Bamburgh

The route runs inland for several miles south of Bamburgh towards Dunstanburgh as the coastal option is either a busy road (the B1340) or a footpath. (Sustrans are currently trying to negotiate a better coastal route between Bamburgh, Seahouses and Beadnell). There are nevertheless views out to sea and the lighthouse on Farne Islands and a chance to divert to Seahouses, an unashamed holiday resort village about five miles south of Bamburgh.

Chathill Station, one of those 1950s throwback stations with only two stopping trains a day, lies along delightful, quiet, flat lanes between arable fields. There is a splendid pub about two miles off the route at Low Newton-by-the-Sea, from which there are marvellous walks along the huge sandy beaches.

South of Embleton, ever-better views emerge of the dramatic ruins of Dunstanburgh Castle, which can only be reached on foot. An excellent concrete track between Dunstan Steads and Dunstan Square takes you past a series of pill boxes made of petrified sand bags, a defence precaution against German invasion in the Second World War.

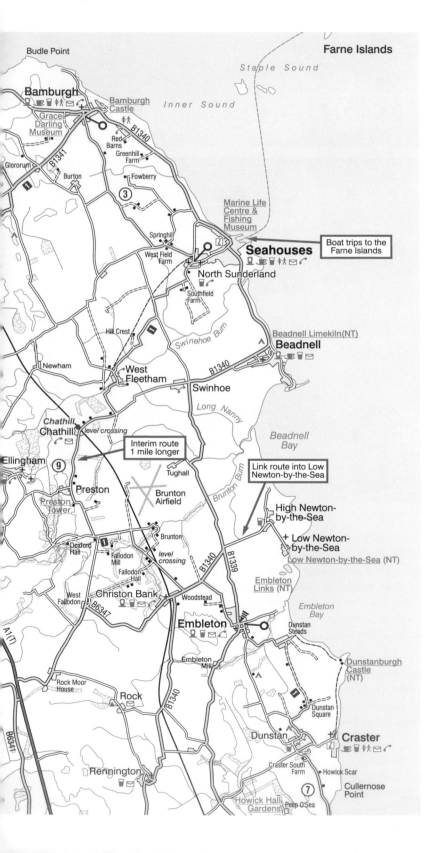

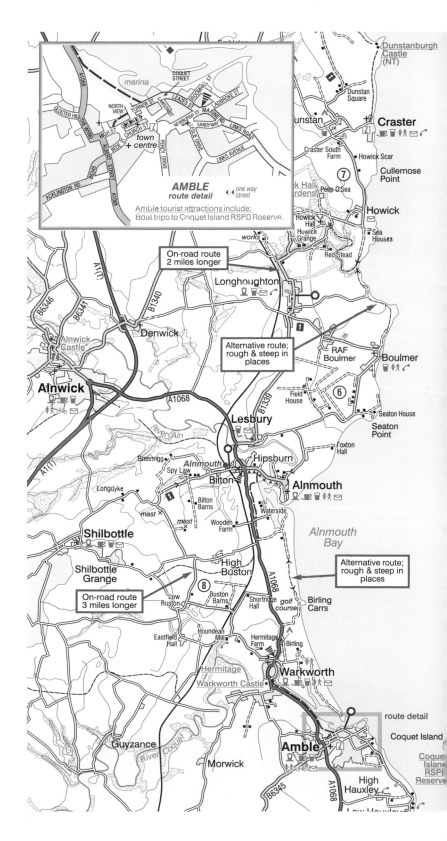

AMBLE
route detail ‹‹ one way street

Amble tourist attractions include:
Boat trips to Coquet Island RSPB Reserve.

On-road route 2 miles longer

Alternative route; rough & steep in places

Alternative route; rough & steep in places

On-road route 3 miles longer

Along the coast south of Craster

Craster is famous for smoked fish, courtesy of Robsons & Sons, fish curers, but it also has a lovely little harbour, a village shop, the Jolly Fisherman Inn and Bark Pots Tearoom. South of here, you have a choice. A rough but spectacular coastal ride, using a track which is occasionally bumpy, stony, grassy, sandy and steep, is well worth doing on a fine day for the wild beauty of the coastline, even if you have to walk some sections. The alternative inland route takes you via Longhoughton, a service village for the nearby RAF base at Boulmer.

Approaching Alnmouth, you see the last few winding turns of the River Aln, at the end of its journey from the eastern slopes of the Cheviots to the sea at Alnmouth. Again, you have a choice of route to reach Warkworth: a rough coastal track with lovely views out to sea or a longer inland route on quiet lanes.

Warkworth is a very attractive village dominated by the ruins of its 12th-century castle, with a broad main street lined with handsome yellow stone houses, galleries, tearooms, pubs and shops. The centre is reached by a lovely old bridge over the River Coquet, which describes a horseshoe shape around the village. If you fancy a change from cycling, you could hire a rowing boat on the Coquet. A new riverside path alongside the A1068 brings you into the back of Amble, near the marina. Be sure to visit Amble harbour, one of the most photogenic of the whole trip.

Looking east towards Alnmouth

GRADE OF DIFFICULTY
Moderate

MAJOR CLIMBS
A gently undulating day, rarely crossing the 50m contour (165ft). The one climb worth mentioning is on the inland route from Alnmouth south to Warkworth – 360ft (110m) west through Bilton to the radio mast.

PUBLIC TRANSPORT
Trains from Alnmouth to Berwick and Newcastle, depart approximately every 1½ to 2 hours from 8am to 8pm Monday to Friday, but with a reduced service at the weekends. See day ride page 59.

NATIONAL RAIL ENQUIRIES
08457 48 49 50

ARRIVA TRAINS NORTHERN
0870 602 3322
www.arrivatrainsnorthern.co.uk

TOURIST INFORMATION

SEAHOUSES (SEASONAL)
01665 720884

ADDERSTONE, NEAR BELFORD
01668 213678

CRASTER (SEASONAL)
01665 576007

ALNWICK
01665 510665

AMBLE (SEASONAL)
01665 712313

BIKE SHOPS

AMBLE

BREEZE'S BIKES
(Cycle hire)
Coquet Street
01665 710323

PEDAL POWER CYCLE HIRE
(Cycle hire only)
22 Hauxley Way
01665 710323

SEAHOUSES

SEAHOUSES CYCLE HIRE
(Cycle hire only)
4 Broad Road
01665 721066 or 07947 169163

PLACES OF INTEREST

BAMBURGH
See page 59

DUNSTANBURGH CASTLE
01665 576231
The ruins of the 14th century castle (1 mile off the route) are set on a 100ft cliff and are accessible only on foot, either from Dunstan Steads, from the north or from Craster, from the south. The castle has a massive keep and a long line of towers along the perimeter wall.

CRASTER
This unspoilt fishing village, built of the local dark whinstone, is famous for its oak-smoked kippers. The herrings used are not caught locally, although you can sample a sandwich of locally caught crab! If you plan to visit Dunstanburgh Castle there is a splendid walk of just over a mile from Craster along the coast to the spectacular ruins.

HOWICK HALL
The trees in Howick Hall gardens shelter colourful banks of plants and shrubs. A path runs through a wooded valley down to the shoreline and Rumbling Kern gully.

WARKWORTH
The village is enclosed by a horseshoe loop of the River Coquet. The shell of the castle (01665 711423) stands at the top of the main street.

AMBLE
The village was a coal harbour and is now a fishing port with fine views up the estuary towards

Rainbow near Howick

Warkworth Castle. Half a mile upstream from the medieval hump-backed bridge is the 14th-century hermitage, with a tiny vaulted chapel built into the cliff.

REFRESHMENTS
There are plenty of places to choose from in Seahouses (just off the route), Alnmouth, Warkworth and Amble.

In smaller villages, try:

Bamburgh – Lord Crewe Arms pub, Victoria Hotel, Copper Kettle tearooms, shops

Low Newton by the Sea (just off the route) – the Ship pub

Embleton – Dunstanburgh Castle Hotel, Sportsman Hotel, Grey's Inn (also does teas and coffees)

Dunstan – Cottage Inn

Craster (just off the route) – Jolly Fisherman pub, Bark Pots tearoom, shop

Longhoughton – village shop

Boulmer – Burneside Inn

ACCOMMODATION

SEAHOUSES

WESTFIELD FARMHOUSE
North Sunderland
01665 720161
www.westfieldfarmhouse.co.uk

RAILSTON HOUSE
133 Main Street
01665 720912
www.railstonehouse.net

EMBLETON

BLUE BELL INN
01665 576573

SPORTSMAN INN
Sea Lane
01665 576588

BRUNTON HOUSE
01665 589198
victoria@joliffe326.fsnet.co.uk

CRASTER

THE COTTAGE INN
Dunstan Village (west of Craster)
01665 576658

HOWICK SCAR FARMHOUSE
(south of Craster)
01665 576665
www.howickscar.co.uk

ALNMOUTH

BEECH LODGE
8 Alnwood
01665 830709

WESTLEA
29 Riverside Road
01665 830730
email:
janiceedwards@totalise.co.uk

THE GRANGE
Northumberland Street
01665 830401
www.thegrange-alnmouth.com

SADDLE HOTEL
24 / 25 Northumberland Street
01665 830476
www.accta.co.uk

BILTON BARNS
(west of the railway station)
01665 830427
www.biltonbarns.co.uk

HIPSBURN FARM
01665 830206
www.hipsburnfarmhouse.com

WARKWORTH

SUN HOTEL
6 Castle Terrace
01665 711259

BECK AND CALL
Birling West Cottage
01665 711653
www.beck-n-call.co.uk

ROXBRO HOUSE
5 Castle Terrace
01665 711416
roxbrohouse@aol.com

THE OLD MANSE
20 The Butts
01665 710850

BED & BREAKFAST
7 Woodlands
01665 711263
www.accta.co.uk/north

AMBLE

AMBLE INN
16 Leazes Street
01665 714661

MARINE HOUSE
20 Marine Road
01665 711965

COQUETSIDE
16 Broomhill Street
01665 710352

THE HOLLIES
3 Riverside Park
01665 712323
www.the-hollies-amble.co.uk

DRURIDGE BAY
(South of Amble)

CRESSWELL HOUSE
Cresswell Village
01670 861302
www.s-h-
systems.co.uk/hotels/cresswell

Route along Druridge Bay, South of Amble

Amble to Newcastle

40 miles
Moderate
Follow Coast and Castles, Route 1 and
Hadrian's Cycleway, Route 72

This may be the final stage of your trip if you are completing the loop from Newcastle to Haltwhistle and Berwick. If so, you will see a great contrast today between urban industrial landscapes and rural agricultural landscapes. And – uniquely – there is one stretch, from leaving the pretty village of Creswell to the start of the dunes at the southern edge of Blyth, where it's probably better not to take your time and savour the scenery, but put your head down and cover the miles.

Heading south from Amble, you soon leave tarmac and go onto a good stone-based bridleway. The coastline is followed closely, on track and tarmac, for the next 10 miles. The signposting here is somewhat sporadic, so keep your eyes open for any sign with a bike on it! Passing through a series of nature reserves (with two visitor centres) in the early part of the ride, you are in a landscape of dunes beneath huge skies. Away in the distance, the chimneys of the aluminium works in Lynemouth remind you that this wild, coastal part of the ride will finish all too soon. From Lynemouth southwards, there is no alternative to the route alongside the busy and noisy A189, then a very bitty route through the back streets of Blyth. It is not dangerous, as you are either on segregated cyclepaths or quiet streets, but it is not scenic either. After just over 10 miles, you will be back by the sea and the dunes leading to Seaton Sluice.

A new path starting after the Delaval Arms pub leads to the coast with glorious views to St Mary's Lighthouse. This is the last section of open coastline before the start of the long urban section through Whitley Bay and Tynemouth, then along the River Tyne into the heart of Newcastle.

The ride through Whitley Bay, which should be straightforward, is somewhat confusing. Of the many flat paths on different levels close to the sea, some are pavements, some end in steps and some end on the beach. So keep a sharp eye out for signs, trying to look ahead for the end of each new section of path. This is not somewhere to rush through, particularly in summer when there will be hundreds of people strolling along the promenade.

A signpost beneath the priory and castle in Tynemouth indicates the end of the C2C route and the start of Hadrian's Way. Follow Hadrian's (cycle) way, route 72 into Newcastle. This route climbs up from Fish Quay and the fish markets and generally stays above the River Tyne with great views out over the shipyards' cranes. The route ends where it began, under the bridges over the River Tyne, in the heart of Newcastle. Congratulations! Why not come back and try some of the day rides described in the second half of this book?

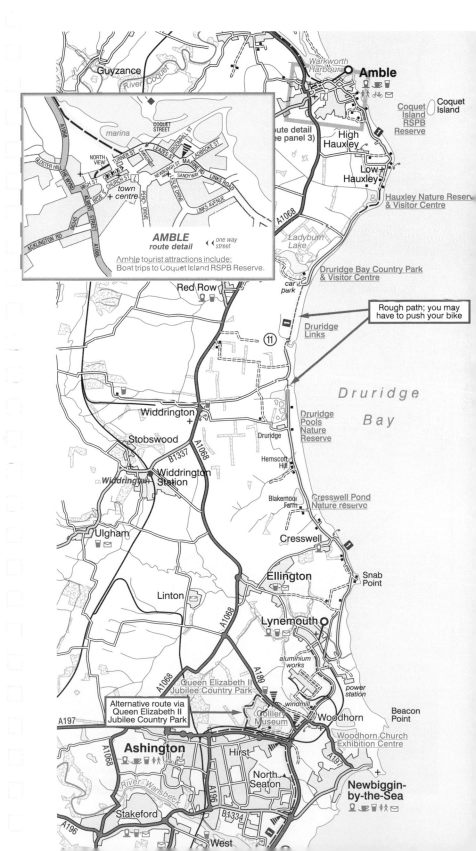

Guyzance

River Coquet

Warkworth Harbour

Amble

Coquet Island

Coquet Island RSPB Reserve

route detail (see panel 3)

High Hauxley

Low Hauxley

Hauxley Nature Reserve & Visitor Centre

AMBLE route detail

‹‹ one way street

Amble tourist attractions include: Boat trips to Coquet Island RSPB Reserve.

marina

COQUET STREET

NORTH VIEW

GLOSTER HILL THE WYND

HIGH ST

ALBERT STREET

ACKLINGTON RD

B6345

A1068

TURNER ST

LEAZES ST

BROOMHILL ST

MOBROKE ST

QUEEN ST

CHURCH ST

NEWBURGH ST

MARINE RD

SANDY WAY

LESLIE DRIVE

PERCY DRIVE

LINKS ROAD

LINKS DRIVE

LINKS AVENUE

town centre

Ladyburn Lake

A1068

Druridge Bay Country Park & Visitor Centre

car park

Red Row

Druridge Links

(11)

Rough path; you may have to push your bike

Druridge Bay

Widdrington

Stobswood

Druridge

Druridge Pools Nature Reserve

Hemscott Hill

B1337

A1068

Widdrington Station

Blakemoor Farm

Cresswell Pond Nature reserve

Ulgham

Cresswell

Snab Point

Ellington

Linton

A1068

Lynemouth

aluminium works

A189

power station

Queen Elizabeth II Jubilee Country Park

A1068

windmill

Alternative route via Queen Elizabeth II Jubilee Country Park

A197

Colliery Museum

Woodhorn

Beacon Point

Woodhorn Church Exhibition Centre

Ashington

Hirst

A1068

A189

North Seaton

A197

River Wansbeck

A196

Newbiggin-by-the-Sea

Stakeford

A196

B1334

West

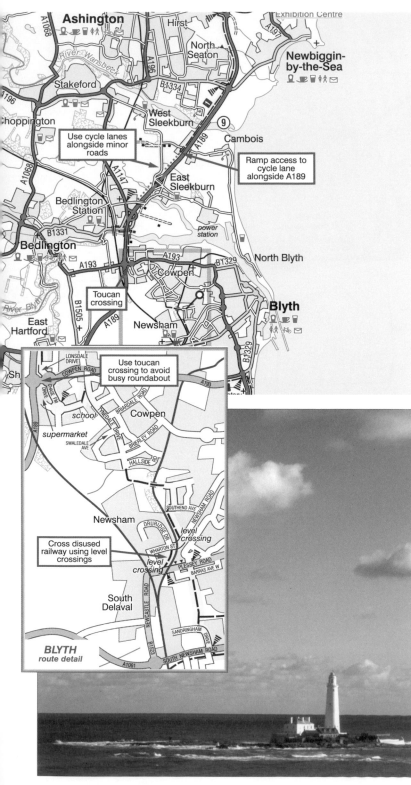

St. Mary's Island and lighthouse

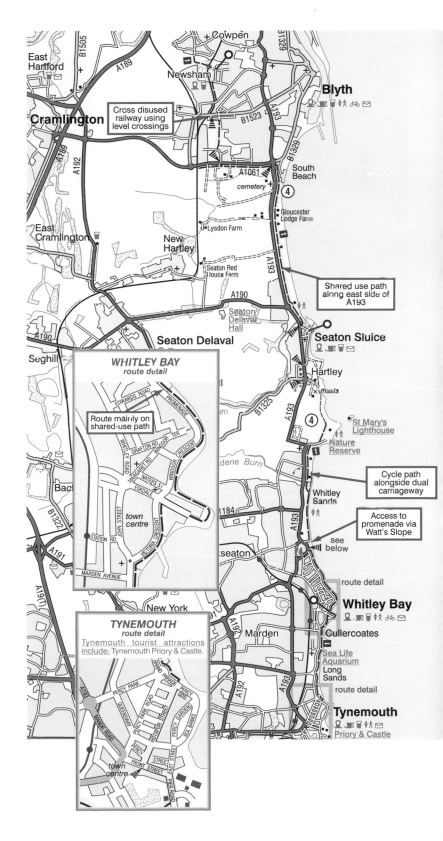

Cowpen

East Hartford

Newsham

Blyth

Cramlington

Cross disused railway using level crossings

South Beach

cemetery

④

East Cramlington

New Hartley

Lysdon Farm

Gloucester Lodge Farm

Seaton Red House Farm

A190

Shared use path along east side of A193

Seaton Delaval Hall

Seghill

Seaton Delaval

Seaton Sluice

Hartley

×masts

WHITLEY BAY
route detail

EDWARDS ROAD

PROMENADE

Route mainly on shared-use path

GRAFTON RD

WHITLEY ROAD

MARGARET RD

WINDSOR TER

WINDSOR CRESCENT

NATERS ST

ESKDALE

Bac

JOHN STREET

town centre

STATION RD

VICTORIA CRESCENT

MARDEN AVENUE

St Mary's Lighthouse

Nature Reserve

Cycle path alongside dual carriageway

Whitley Sands

Access to promenade via Watt's Slope

see below

route detail

seaton

Whitley Bay

New York

TYNEMOUTH
route detail
Tynemouth tourist attractions include: Tynemouth Priory & Castle.

GRAND PARADE

PERCY PARK

PERCY PARK ROAD

QUEENSWAY

MANOR ROAD

PERCY GDNS

HOTSPUR STREET

WINDSOR STREET

PERCY GARDENS

SEA BANKS

PERCY

FRONT STREET

STREET

EAST STREET

town centre

Marden

Cullercoates

Sea Life Aquarium

Long Sands

route detail

Tynemouth

Priory & Castle

View towards Cullercoats and Whitley Bay

GRADE OF DIFFICULTY
Moderate

MAJOR CLIMBS
None

PUBLIC TRANSPORT
Virgin and GNER operate several trains a day between Newcastle (or Berwick) and Alnmouth, departing approximately every 1 ½ to 2 hours from 0800 to 2000 hrs from Monday to Friday but with a considerably reduced weekend service. It is possible to cut inland to Morpeth, southwest of Lynemouth, for trains to Newcastle if you are short of time.

NATIONAL RAIL ENQUIRIES
08457 48 49 50

ARRIVA TRAINS NORTHERN
0870 602 3322
www.arrivatrainsnorthern.co.uk

TOURIST INFORMATION
ALNWICK
01665 510665

AMBLE (SEASONAL)
01665 712313

WHITLEY BAY
0191 200 8535

NEWCASTLE UPON TYNE
Central Station 0191 230 0030
City centre 0191 277 8000

BIKE SHOPS

AMBLE

BREEZE'S BIKES
(Cycle hire)
Coquet Street
01665 710323

PEDAL POWER CYCLE HIRE
(Cycle hire only)
22 Hauxley Way
01665 710323

ASHINGTON

GEARED UP CYCLE SPORTS
46 Woodhorn Road
01670 812852

TWO WHEEL CITY
71 Station Road
01670 819494

BEDLINGTON

JIM'S CYCLES
1a Front Street West
01670 828464

BEDLINGTON STATION

IAN GERRARD CYCLES
Stone House, Bank Top
01670 823343

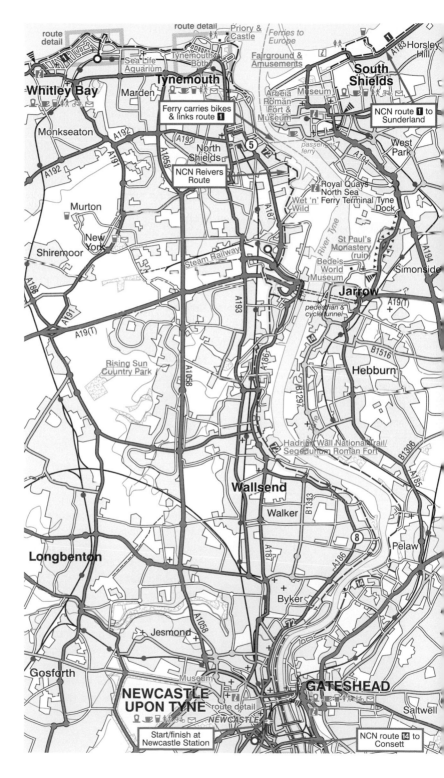

route detail

route detail

Priory & Castle

Ferries to Europe

Fairground & Amusements

Sea Life Aquarium

Tynemouth Both

Tynemouth

Whitley Bay

Marden

Arbeia Roman Fort & Museum

Museum

South Shields

Monkseaton

A192

Ferry carries bikes & links route **1**

North Shields

5

passenger ferry

NCN route **1** to Sunderland

West Park

A194

A192

A191

A192

NCN Reivers Route

A187

Royal Quays North Sea Ferry Terminal / Tyne Dock

Murton

Wet 'n' Wild

A194

Shiremoor

New York

Steam Railway

St Paul's Monastery (ruin)

Bede's World Museum

Simonside

A186

A191

A19(T)

A193

Jarrow

A19(T)

pedestrian & cycle tunnel

B1516

Rising Sun Country Park

A1058

A186

B1297

Hebburn

Hadrian's Wall National Trail / Segedunum Roman Fort

B1306

A185

Longbenton

Wallsend

Walker

B1313

8

Pelaw

A187

A186

14

Byker

A1058

Jesmond

Gosforth

Museum

NEWCASTLE UPON TYNE

route detail

NEWCASTLE

GATESHEAD

Saltwell

Start/finish at Newcastle Station

NCN route **14** to Consett

BLYTH

TWO WHEEL CITY
27 Regent Street
01670 540053

FERGUSONS MOTORS AND CYCLES
16 Union Street
01670 352218

SEATON DELAVAL

DELAVAL CYCLES
180 Astley Road
0191 237 7327

WHITLEY BAY

DIXON'S CYCLES
184 Park View
0191 253 2035

DTS CYCLES
55 Ilfracombe Gardens
0191 251 4667

NORTH SHIELDS

LAVERICK'S CYCLES
22 Station Road, Cullercoats
0191 252 4491

SPOKES
38-39 Nile Street
0191 2962840

Tynemouth Priory

NEWCASTLE

CYCLE CENTRE
250 Shields Road
Byker
0191 265 1472

EDINBURGH BICYCLE CO-OP
5-7 Union Road
Byker
0191 265 8619

PLACES OF INTEREST

AMBLE
See page 65

WOODHORN
01670 856968
There is a colliery museum in the
Queen Elizabeth II Country Park,
with displays of mining and social
history.

NEWBIGGIN BY THE SEA
A worthwhile detour if time allows.
Newbiggin has an attractive beach
and Promenade and plenty of
services.

SEATON DELAVAL HALL
(¾ mile off the route along the
A190)
Designed by Sir John Vanbrugh,
the interior of this 18th-century
mansion includes a superb
sculpted chimneypiece in the Great
Hall. The Norman chapel in the
grounds houses family tombs and
14th-century effigies.

WHITLEY BAY
Seafront hotels and guesthouses
overlook flower gardens along the
resort's promenade. If your legs
can take the 137 steps to the top of
St Mary's lighthouse you will be
rewarded with great coastal views,
0191 200 8650

TYNEMOUTH
The seafront is dominated by the
walls of the 1090 Norman church,
later fortified by Richard II. The

Leaving St Mary's Island and lighthouse

Enjoing the sea views

timber watch house of the volunteer life brigade holds a small museum illustrating local off-shore wrecks and rescues.

WALLSEND

The town grew up where Hadrian's Wall reached the sea.

NEWCASTLE

A fine city and fitting place to have started, and now to end your journey. After your time spent in splendid rural isolation, cycling around Northumberland, the urban bustle and variety of shops, restaurants, pubs and bars will be a major contrast (sample the famous Geordie nightlife on the Quayside or Bigg Market). It is well worth planning a days stay in the city before heading home.

Historical highlights include Grey Street and Grainger Town architecture, the Castle Keep and St. Nicholas' Cathedral. In contrast to the historic parts of the city, there's also Newcastle and neighbouring Gateshead's

The Millennium Bridge and the Baltic Arts Centre, Gateshead

redeveloped Quayside areas where you will find the contemporary Baltic Arts Centre, Sage Music Centre and elegant Millennium Bridge sitting next to the old Quayside area, with its medieval origins.

The city centre is compact enough to cover on foot (or by bike) but large enough to boast a selection of art galleries, museums, theatres and cinemas, so there should be more than enough to keep you busy!

REFRESHMENTS

There are plenty of places to choose from in Amble, Whitley Bay, Tynemouth and Newcastle.

Druridge Bay - Cafe at the Druridge Bay Visitor Centre

Cresswell - Ice Cream shop and just north of Cresswell The Drift Inn Cafe

Seaton Sluice - Delaval Arms pub

ACCOMMODATION

WHITLEY BAY

THE MARLBOROUGH HOTEL

20-21 East Parade
0191 251 3628
www.marlborough-hotel.com

YORK HOUSE HOTEL

30 Park Parade
0191 252 8313
email: reservations
@yorkhousehotel.com

CHERRYTREE HOUSE

35 Brook Street
0191 251 4306
email: cherrytreehouse@
cherrytreehouse.free-online.co.uk

NEWCASTLE

For details of accommodation in Newcastle city centre see page 19. Alternatively here are the relevant Tourist Information Centres.
0191 277 8000 (Grainger Street)
0191 230 0030 (Central Station)

Day Rides

1 Haltwhistle & Lambley Viaduct - The South Tyne Trail

The traffic-free railway path south from Haltwhistle to the spectacular Lambley Viaduct is a rarity in Northumberland, where there are very few dismantled railways converted to recreational use in contrast to neighbouring County Durham. So make the most of this excellent ride, which climbs gently up the valley of the River South Tyne, through a rolling landscape of drystone walls, pasture and copses of deciduous trees, with fine views towards the North Pennines. There is a chance of refreshment

Lambley Viaduct

at the Wallace Arms, either on your outward or return trip. You may wish simply to go out and back on the railway path or, as an alternative, use the quiet lanes that take you down past Featherstone Castle (a haunted castle with parts dating back to the 14th century). A short section alongside the River South Tyne leads to the only noticeable climb of the ride, setting you up for a fine descent back to Haltwhistle.

START POINT AND DISTANCE
Haltwhistle Railway station
10 miles

GRADE OF DIFFICULTY
Easy / moderate (easy if you ride there and back on the railway path).

MAJOR CLIMBS
There is a gentle climb of 260ft (80m) over 5 miles from the crossing of the River South Tyne to Lambley Viaduct, and one short steep hill on the return, a climb up from the riverside section after Featherstone Castle.

PUBLIC TRANSPORT
Regular train service to Haltwhistle. Hadrian's Wall Bus has cycle

carriage (01434 322002 for information).

TOURIST INFORMATION
HALTWHISTLE
01434 322002

BIKE SHOPS
EDEN'S LAWN SERVICE STATION
(cycle hire and spares only)
Bypass Road, Haltwhistle
01434 320443

THE BIKE SHOP
17 Westgate, Haltwhistle
01434 322544

REFRESHMENTS
Haltwhistle - lots of choice
Rowfoot - Wallace Arms pub

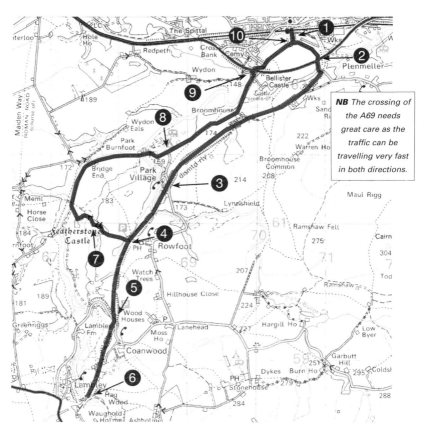

NB *The crossing of the A69 needs great care as the traffic can be travelling very fast in both directions.*

ROUTE INSTRUCTIONS

1. Go out of Haltwhistle railway station, turn right then first right again, signposted 'Alston, Route 68'. Cross the bridge over the river and turn left.

2. Take extreme care at the A69 crossing. Go straight ahead onto the lane opposite, then shortly turn right, onto the railway path.

3. After 2 miles, go straight ahead at the first road crossing.

4. Go straight ahead at the second road crossing and car park. The Wallace Arms pub is 100 yards uphill to the left.

5. Go straight ahead at the third road crossing and car park, signposted 'Lambley Viaduct', leaving the Pennine Cycleway (Route 68).

6. Go to the end of the viaduct, turn round and retrace your steps as far as the second road crossing. Route instruction 4 on map. Wallace Arms pub up to the right). Turn left here.

7. Climb gently then go steeply downhill, passing the castle on the left. Keep the water to your left (ie ignore the bridge that crosses the river).

8. At the T-junction at the top of the climb turn left, signposted 'Haltwhistle 1¾'.

9. After 1¼ miles, turn left just before the main road (A69), taking the left-hand (concrete) track, signposted 'Public Bridleway to Haltwhistle'.

10. Go under the bridge, follow the road to the right then take the second left to recross the green metal bridge and return to Haltwhistle.

2 Haltwhistle to Hadrian's Wall

Hadrian's Wall

This ride gives you the chance to walk a section of Hadrian's Wall and visit the Roman Army Museum at Walltown. Leaving the handsome town of Haltwhistle, you climb steeply up on a narrow lane alongside Haltwhistle Burn up to Lees Hall Farm. The ever-better views behind to the North Pennines are as good an excuse as any to take a breather! The tarmac runs out at the farm and there is a short section on a stone track, which may be muddy after rain. At this point you cross the B6318 - the Military Road. Historical records suggest that the road was built by General Wade as part of efforts to quell the Scottish Jacobite rebellion in 1745. It is thought to run along the top of the foundation course of Hadrian's Wall for more than six miles, probably using stone from the wall itself. Across the Military Road is a minor lane opposite, which once again turns into a wide track across land grazed by livestock. About a mile after rejoining tarmac you come to the Roman Army Museum, where you may choose to stop for a while and walk along the wall towards Walltown or, in the other direction, towards Thirlwall Castle or the pub at Greenhead. You have done your climbing for the day and can now enjoy a long descent all the way back.

START POINT AND DISTANCE
Haltwhistle Railway Station
7 ½ miles.

GRADE OF DIFFICULTY
Moderate, with some rough surfaces

MAJOR CLIMBS
There is a 295ft (90m) climb, at

times steep, from the start up to Lees Hall Farm.

PUBLIC TRANSPORT
Regular train service to Haltwhistle

TOURIST INFORMATION
HALTWHISTLE
01434 322002

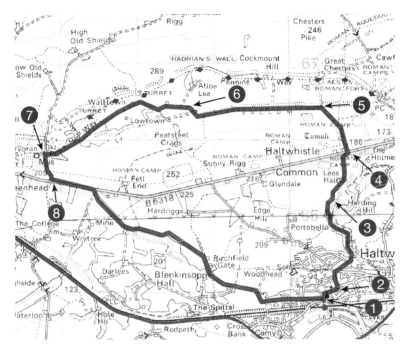

BIKE SHOPS

EDEN'S LAWN SERVICE STATION

(cycle hire and spares only)
Bypass Road, Haltwhistle
01434 320443

THE BIKE SHOP

17 Westgate, Haltwhistle
01434 322544

REFRESHMENTS

Haltwhistle - lots of choice

ROUTE INSTRUCTIONS

1 Go out of Haltwhistle Station
   and continue straight ahead,
   following 'Route 68' and
   'Route 72' signs.

2 Turn left onto Aesica Road,
   opposite Westgate Wine Store
   and just before the Sandwich
   Bar. Shortly, at the T-junction,
   turn right then first left, onto
   Willia Road.

3 Descend, then climb steeply.
   The tarmac turns to track at the
   third gate, at the end of Lees
   Hall Farm.

4 At the end of the track, at the

T-junction with the road, turn
right, then left. Take care as
there is often fast traffic on the
Military Road (B6318).

5 Follow the broad stone track
   through gates and across
   pasture as it swings left.

6 At the T-junction with tarmac,
   bear left to continue in the
   same direction.

7 At the T-junction, with the car
   park ahead and a no through
   road to the right, turn left*.
   *This is a good place to lock
   up your bike, visit the Roman
   Army Museum and / or go for a
   walk beside Hadrian's Wall by
   Walltown or down to Thirlwall
   Castle or Greenhead, where
   there is a pub.*

8 (Return to Haltwhistle). At the
   T-junction with the B6318 (the
   Military Road), turn left. Take
   care on this busy road. After ¼
   mile take the first right and
   follow for 2 miles back into
   Haltwhistle.

3 Haltwhistle to Bardon Mill and Plenmeller Common

This is by far the toughest of the three rides from Haltwhistle and is only suitable for mountain bikes. You follow the Tyne east for 5 miles, from Haltwhistle to Bardon Mill, before a footbridge over the river drops you close to Beltingham, a village with long associations with the Bowes Lyons family. The late Queen Elizabeth, the Queen Mother, visited frequently. Beltingham lies at the bottom of a long and steep climb onto the remoteness of Plenmeller Common, with far-reaching views north over the Tyne Valley and south-east down into Allendale. Plenmeller Common was a major opencast mine between 1991 and 1998, producing almost 2 million tons of coal. Since its closure, major reclamation work has taken place, involving the replacement of earth and a top layer of peat. After making your way across the bleak summit, you are rewarded with a fantastic long and fast descent back to Haltwhistle.

Steep wooded climb above Beltingham

River Tyne near Haltwhistle

START POINT AND DISTANCE
Haltwhistle Railway Station
10 miles

GRADE OF DIFFICULTY
Strenuous, both for the hills and
the rough surface on top of
Plenmeller Common.

MAJOR CLIMBS
One long climb, at times steep, of
690ft (210m) from the crossing of
the River Tyne at Bardon Mill to the
top of Plenmeller Common. The
steep section goes on for about 1½
miles between Route Instructions 4
and 5.

PUBLIC TRANSPORT
Regular train services to
Haltwhistle from Newcastle and
Carlisle.

TOURIST INFORMATION
HALTWHISTLE
01434 322002

BIKE SHOPS
EDEN'S LAWN SERVICE STATION
(cycle hire and spares only)
Bypass Road
Haltwhistle
01434 320443

THE BIKE SHOP
17 Westgate, Haltwhistle
01434 322544

REFRESHMENTS
Haltwhistle - lots of choice

ROUTE INSTRUCTIONS
1 Go out of Haltwhistle Station
   and continue straight ahead at
   the crossroads, following
   'Route 68' and 'Route 72' signs
   through town, under the A69
   bypass and along the minor
   road running parallel with the
   main road, the railway line and
   the river.

2 After 3 miles, at the T-junction
   in Henshaw, turn right to go
   through Redburn and Bardon
   Mill.

3 After 1 mile, immediately after the war memorial on your right, turn right down a no-through-road (opposite the lane where Route 68 and 72 go left). Cross the bridge over the river and turn left.

4 After 1¼ miles, at the T-junction by the telephone box, turn right, signposted 'Whitfield 4¾'.

5 Long steep climb over almost 2 miles. Where the road turns left for Whitfield, continue straight ahead onto a no-through-road.

6 Continue in the same direction, ignoring right turns to farms as the tarmac turns to track. Go straight ahead, signposted 'Public Byway, Plenmeller Common'.

7 About ½ mile after the summit the grassy track ends and you join a new stone track. As track swings left, bear right (in effect straight ahead) through a gate. Short, very rough section. The path veers right and eventually you will see on the horizon a house, and the road you have to join.

8 At the road, turn right. Fast descent. Take great care as you cross the A69 onto the road diagonally opposite. After ¼ mile, turn right over the bridge to return to Haltwhistle Station.

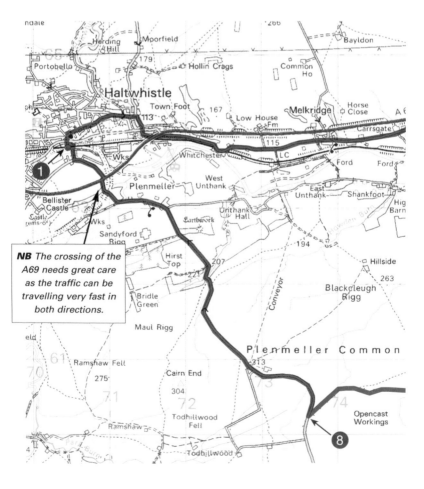

NB *The crossing of the A69 needs great care as the traffic can be travelling very fast in both directions.*

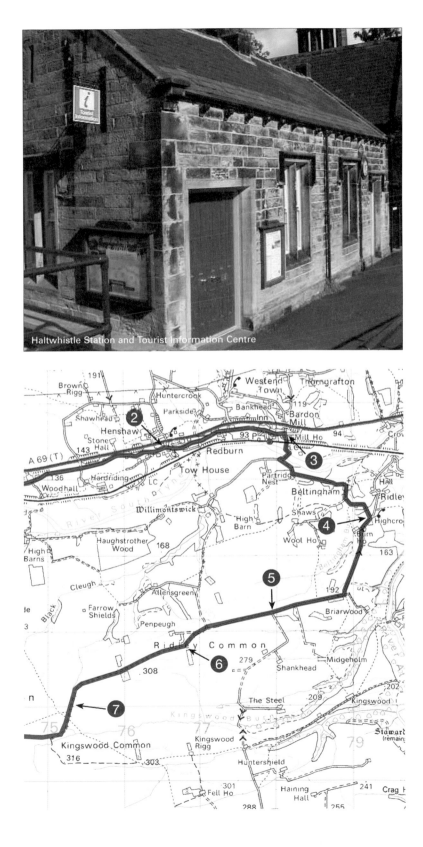

Haltwhistle Station and Tourist Information Centre

4 Bellingham to Wark and Gunnerton

This ride climbs in and out of valleys formed by the River North Tyne and its tributaries, including the Rede, Warks Burn, Gofton Burn and the delightfully-named Houxty Burn, all lying to the south and east of Bellingham (pronounced 'Bellinjum'). The ride uses some of the quietest roads in the region – you'd be unlucky to see a dozen cars in as many miles after leaving the B6320 south of Bellingham and rejoining it to the south of Wark. After leaving Bellingham, you pass along a lovely line of beech and sycamore trees through a countryside of pasture and woodland, bounded by stone walls, with views to the hills to the north of the Tyne Valley. Stone-built farms and barns dot the landscape. The area is dominated by forestry and there are views west towards Kielder, by far the largest forest in all of England. A few miles after the hamlet of Stonehaugh, you come to one of the highlights of the ride: the lovely gated road through broadleaf woodland alongside Gofton Burn. Wark is your only chance of refreshment on the whole ride. You should be able to catch glimpses of Chipchase Castle through the trees to the south-east of Wark. A long steady climb to a high point of almost 900ft (275m) sets you up for a fantasic long descent into Bellingham.

STARTING POINT AND DISTANCE
The Main Square, Bellingham
31 miles

GRADE OF DIFFICULTY
Moderate / strenuous

MAJOR CLIMBS
1 From the bridge over the North Tyne near Bellingham to the top of Ealhamrigg Commom there is a climb of 440ft (134m).
2 A 230ft (70m) climb follows the crossing of Houxty Burn.
3 The longest climb (650ft / 200m) starts at the crossing of Gunnerton Burn and continues for almost 7 miles.

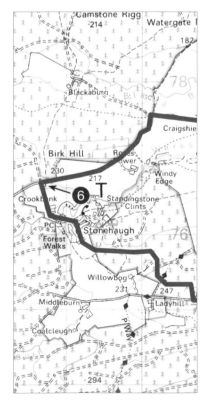

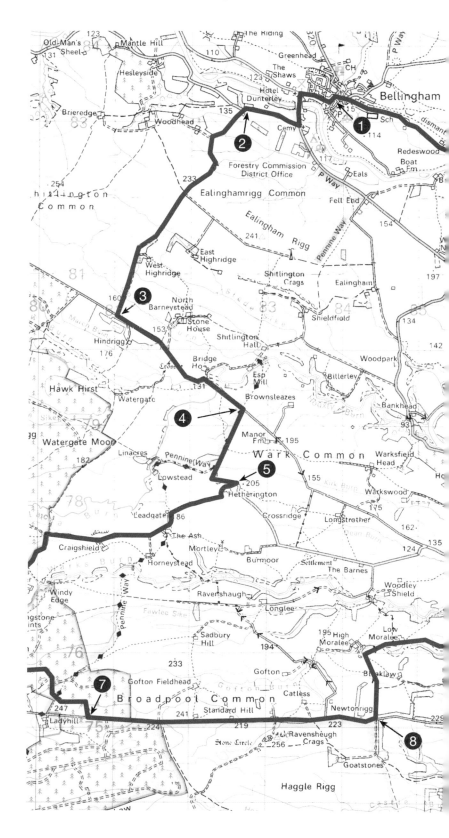

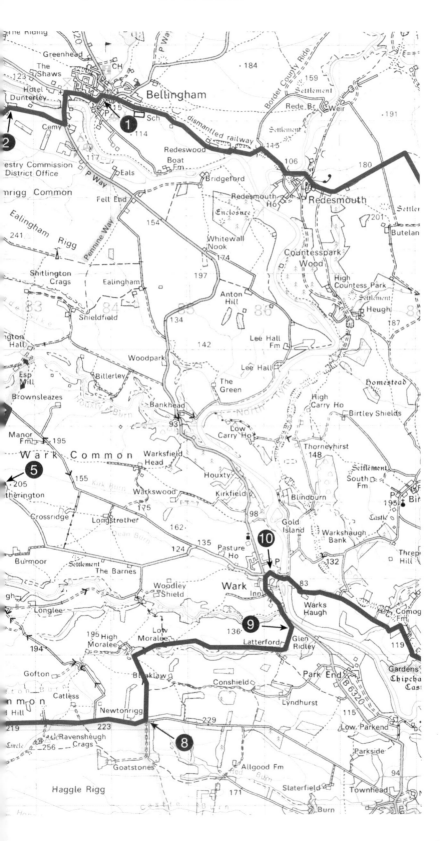

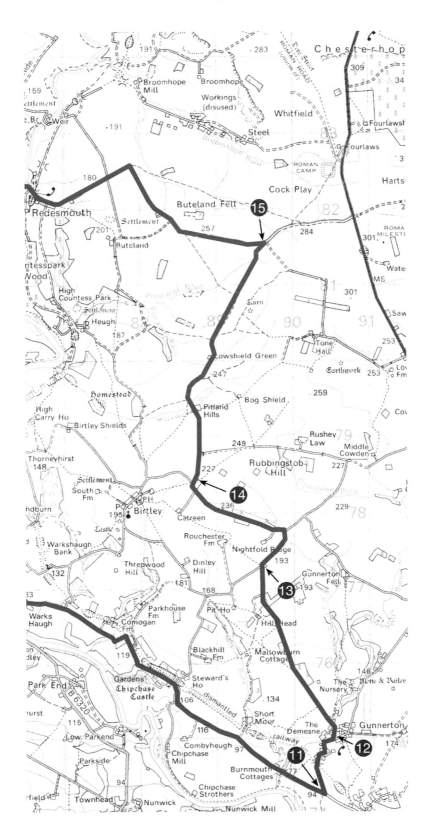

Church in Bellingham

PUBLIC TRANSPORT

Hexham train station is about 10 miles south of Gunnerton, mostly via quiet lanes.

Tyne Valley Coaches service 880 operates from Hexham to Bellingham. There is cycle carriage on this service and it is advisable to book in advance (01434 602217). The Kielder Bus - service 714 operates from Gateshead to Newcastle - Bellingham - Kielder. Contact Traveline 0870 608 2608 for further information.

TOURIST INFORMATION

BELLINGHAM
01434 220616

HEXHAM
01434 652220

BIKE SHOPS

VILLAGE & COUNTRY STORE, BELLINGHAM
(Limited spares only)
01434 220027

REFRESHMENTS

Bellingham - lots of choice

Wark - Battlesteads Hotel, Black Bull Inn, shop

ROUTE INSTRUCTIONS

1 Leave Bellingham on the B6320 towards Hexham. Cross the bridge over the River Tyne then turn first right, signposted 'Route 68, Unsuitable for HGVs'.

2 After ½ mile take the first left signposted, 'Route 68, National Byway', leaving Reivers Route 10, which goes straight ahead.

3 Climb steeply on an unfenced road to the top then descend past a small pine plantation on the left. At the T-junction turn left, signposted 'Wark, Hexham,

Junction of the Pennine Cycleway, Reivers route and National Byway

Route 68, National Byway'.

4 After almost 1½ miles take the first tarmac lane to the right* signposted 'Route 68, National Byway'.

Or, for a short cut to Wark, continue straight ahead here.

5 Second climb on unfenced road. At the T-junction by the gate turn right, signposted 'Route 68, Byway'.

6 After 3 miles turn left, signposted 'Stonehaugh', leaving the Pennine Cycleway (which continues ahead).

7 Go through the hamlet of Stonehaugh then, after 1 ½ miles, at the T-junction, turn left, signposted 'National Byway'.

8 Easy to miss. After 2 ½ miles take the second lane on the left, signposted 'High Moralee'. This sign is on the fence, opposite a footpath sign to 'Slatefield Fell'.

9 Descend then climb. After 2 miles, turn left at the T-junction

with the busy B6320 (take care here).

10 In the centre of Wark turn right, signposted 'Birtley, Barrasford'. Go over the bridge and turn right.

11 Easy to miss. After 3 ½ miles turn left, signposted 'Gunnerton ½'.

12 Turn first left in Gunnerton, signposted 'Birtley 3 ¼'.

13 Steady climb over 2 miles. At the T-junction, turn right, signposted 'Colwell, Woodburn' then take the first left, signposted 'Birtley'.

14 On a sharp left-hand bend, with 'Birtley' signposted to the left, turn right, signposted 'Gates'.

15 Climb for 2½ miles. At the T-junction turn sharp left and follow this superb descent for 4 miles back into Bellingham.

5 Rothbury west along Coquetdale

Hills above Coquetdale

This is the only out-and-out mountain bike ride included in the book. It should only be attempted by fit people on mountain bikes, fitted with fat tyres, and preferably after a few dry days in summer or early autumn. The best bit comes near the start of this ride, once you have climbed out of Rothbury onto the tracks high above Coquetdale. These tracks are wide, well-drained and stone-based, the views are stupendous and, after the initial steep climb, you largely maintain your height until the long, fast descent to rejoin tarmac and the lanes through Snitter. There are three further off-road sections: west of Snitter Windyside, south-west of Burradon, and south of Farnham towards Hepple. Each has rough sections and can be muddy after rain and in winter. Beyond Hepple, a quiet lane up above the Coquet valley takes you all the way back to Rothbury.

STARTING POINT AND DISTANCE
High Street, Rothbury
24 miles

GRADE OF DIFFICULTY
Strenuous, mainly because of the rough, off-road sections.

MAJOR CLIMBS
1   The first 525ft (160m) climb out of Rothbury is by far the toughest, with a very steep bridleway section up through the woodland.

2   There are two 200ft (60m) climbs after the two crossings of Foxton Burn: one north to Burradon and one south to Sharperton Edge.

3   A final 165ft (50m) climb above Coquetdale, following the crossing of the river near Hepple.

PUBLIC TRANSPORT

No railway station nearby. Bus services 516 Morpeth - Rothbury - Thropton and 508 Gateshead - Newcastle - Belsay - Rothbury (This is a summer service only). Contact 0870 608 2608 or visit www.jplanner.org.uk for details.

TOURIST INFORMATION

ROTHBURY (SEASONAL)

01669 620887

BIKE SHOPS

SPAR SUPERMARKET

(Cycle hire and spares only)
Main Street, Rothbury
01669 621338

REFRESHMENTS

Rothbury - lots of choice
Pub about 2 miles off the route in **Thropton**

Woodland tracks above Rothbury

ROUTE INSTRUCTIONS

1 From the centre of Rothbury, follow the B6341 west towards Thropton.

2 Towards the end of Rothbury, turn right by St Agnes Catholic Church opposite Rothbury House. Climb steeply and take the second (sharp) right onto Hillside East.

3 Climb then descend. At the end of the row of houses on the left, keep an eye out for a 'Public Bridleway' sign on the left. Climb (or push) through very steep woodland. At the T-junction with the wide stone track, turn left uphill.

4 Leave the woodland and go through the gate onto a landscape of boulders, heather, fern and wide views. Pass to the right of the mast.

5 After almost 2 miles, at a crossroads of tracks with three field gates, turn left uphill onto the track marked 'Forestry Commission. Dogs on leads'.

6 Rejoin tarmac on fast descent. At the crossroads, go straight ahead, signposted 'Netherton, Snitter'.

7 At the fork of lanes in Snitter, bear right. At the T-junction, turn right.

8 After 1 mile, turn first left, signposted 'Windyside, Low Trewhitt'.

9 Go past the farm. At the bottom of the hill, shortly after a sharp, right-hand bend, cross a bridge over a stream then turn immediately left onto a wide stone track.

10 At the T-junction with the road, turn right. Climb, descend, then climb again.

11 Immediately before the 'Burradon' signpost at the start

of the hamlet, turn left, signposted 'Low Burradon'. At the end of the tarmac, do not go left into the farm but continue straight ahead onto the (muddy) track through the gate ahead.

12 Go through two more gates, cross a footbridge over the stream and turn right onto a wide grassy track. Go through a wide, corrugated iron gate and turn left up a rutted grassy track. Follow this round to the right.

13 At the T-junction with the road, turn left.

14 After 1 mile, at the next T-junction, turn left, and after ⅓ mile, take the first right, signposted 'Low Farnham, High Farnham'.

15 Shortly after passing between farm buildings on a sharp left-hand bend, bear right (in effect straight ahead) uphill onto a track signposted, 'Footpath to Caistron'.

16 Go past the farm, over the cattlegrid, and bear right onto the downhill track, signposted 'Offroad Bike Route'.

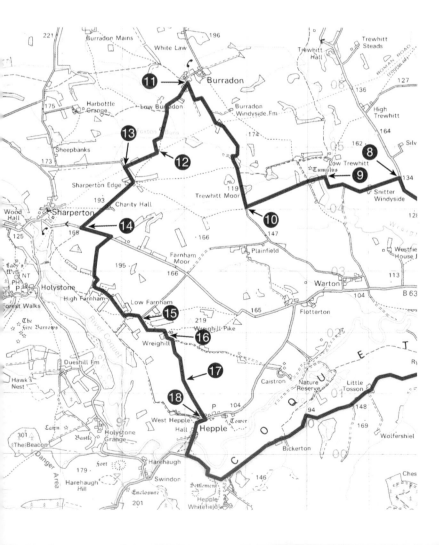

17 As the excellent track swings sharp right at the end of the field, bear left (in effect straight ahead) and go downhill, through the gate, onto a steep wide rutted grass track towards the house at the bottom.

18 At the T-junction with the B6341, turn right, then after ½ mile, on a sharp right-hand bend, turn left, signposted 'Bickerton' Tosson'.

19 Climb for 2 miles. Descend to Ryehill, then follow the lane for a further 2 ½ miles.

20 Shortly after passing a caravan park on the right, turn left downhill, signposted 'Rothbury'.

21 At the T-junction, turn left to cross the bridge over the River Coquet, signposted 'Alnwick, Thropton' to return to the start.

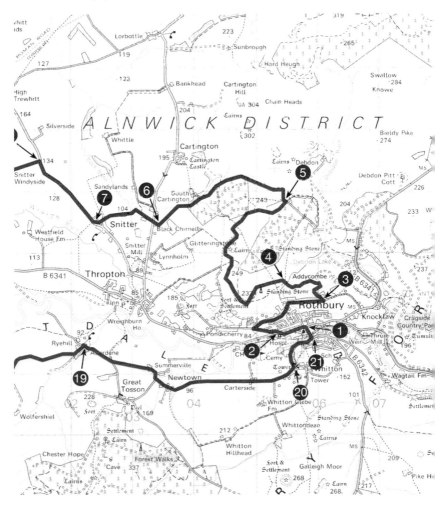

6 Whittingham to Abberwick

Between the Cheviots and the coast there is another low range of hills stretching from Rothbury (Coquetdale) in the south to the Kyloe Hills beyond Belford in the north. The summits rise to 700-1,000 ft (200-300m), reaching a high point of 1,050ft (319m) on Long Crag, in Thrunton Wood, north of Rothbury. This ride from Whittingham explores these hills, passing alongside Thrunton Wood and climbing to a high crossing of the A697, which leads to a wonderful unfenced lane with a real 'roof-of-the-world' feel as it passes the radio mast at Newtown. A long, grassy descent gives you fine views towards Edlingham Castle and the viaduct that used to carry the railway from Alnwick to Coldstream. Beyond the hamlet of Abberwick, the ride drops to cross the River Aln, the only river that cuts through the range of hills between Rothbury and Berwick. The A697 is crossed directly on tiny quiet lanes to take you back to the start point in Whittingham.

Autumn sunshine near Bolton

The Cheviot Hills from Abberwick

STARTING POINT AND DISTANCE
Centre of Whittingham
17 miles

GRADE OF DIFFICULTY
Moderate

MAJOR CLIMBS
1 There are three climbs, each longer than the last, of 115ft (35m), 245ft (75m) and 360ft (110m) in the first 5 miles to get from Whittingham past Thrunton Wood to the masts at the high point.
2 After dropping to cross Edlingham Burn, there is a 360ft (110m) climb to the next high point above Abberwick.

PUBLIC TRANSPORT
The nearest train station is at Alnmouth, about 11 miles to the east of Whittingham, accessible on quiet lanes via Shilbottle. Bus service 473 from Alnwick - Whittingham - Wooler conects with bus services from Newcastle to Alnwick (or cycle from Alnmouth station to Alnwick). The service can offer cycle carriage at off peak times by prior arrangement with the operator IDM Travel on 01668 281578

TOURIST INFORMATION
ALNWICK
01665 510665

ROTHBURY (SEASONAL)
01669 620887

BIKE SHOPS
None on the route.
The nearest is (only for bike hire and spares) Spar Supermarket, Main Street, Rothbury
01669 621338

REFRESHMENTS
None on the route. The nearest is the Queen's Head Pub, shop and cafe, just off the route in **Glanton**.

ROUTE INSTRUCTIONS
1 From the centre of Whittingham, follow signs for 'Alnwick' and 'Whittingham Station'.
2 Climb for ½ mile. On a sharp left-hand bend, bear right (in effect straight ahead) onto a no-through-road, signposted 'Whittingham Lane'.
3 At the farm, go through the gate into the field, descend to a second gate, then climb along the field edge to a third gate.
4 Go through a fourth gate and turn left uphill on a broad, red

gravel track along the edge of the forest then, at the fork of tarmac lanes, bear right uphill.

5 Short descent (with brickworks to the left) then long, steady climb over 2 miles. At the main road, turn sharp left then first right, signposted 'Newtown ¾'.

6 The tarmac lane ends shortly after the farm. Go downhill, along the field edge, on a wide stone and grass track.

7 Where there are two gates side by side, take the right. At the T-junction with the road, turn left.

8 After 2 miles, turn right* at the crossroads by a 'Give Way' sign.

SHORT CUT

> * *Turn left at the crossroads, then go straight ahead at the next crossroads (with the A697) to return to Whittingham.*

9 After ½ mile, ignore the first left on the descent. Cross the bridge and take the next left, signposted 'Abberwick 2'.

10 Steep then steady climb. Take the first left, signposted 'Abberwick, Moorlaws'.

11 Long descent on unfenced road leading to a ford / footbridge at the bottom. About ¾ mile after the ford, at the crossroads by a 'Give Way' sign, turn left, signposted 'Bolton, Glanton'.

12 Easy to miss. After 1½ miles take the second left, opposite the second lodge gate entrance to Shawdon Hall (no road sign).

13 At the crossroads with the A697 go straight ahead, signposted 'Rothill, Middle Barton'.

14 After 1¼ miles, at the T-junction, turn left (no sign) to return to Whittingham.

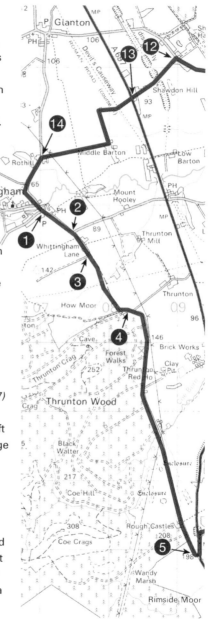

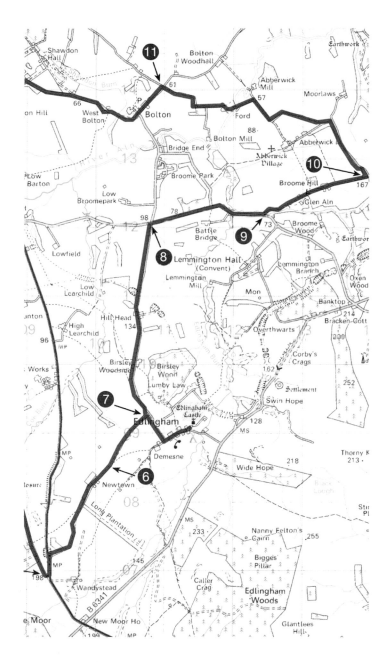

7 Whittingham to Glanton and Ingram

The Plough Inn at Powburn

This short ride at the foot of the Cheviot Hills links the four attractive stone-built villages of Whittingham, Glanton, Powburn and Branton and crosses the River Breamish on a long footbridge that replaced the one swept away by floods a few years ago. You can also veer off to visit the National Park Visitor Centre at Ingram. On the return, the lanes past the lovely buildings of Eslington Park are especially memorable. The infant River Aln is followed back to Whittingham at the start of its long course to the coast at Alnmouth.

STARTING POINT AND DISTANCE
Centre of Whittingham
Full route to Ingram - 16 miles
Short route - 11 miles

GRADE OF DIFFICULTY
Moderate

MAJOR CLIMBS
1   Steady then steep climb of 330ft (100m) north from Whittingham through Glanton to the high point on the slopes of Glanton Hill.
2   A second, shorter climb of 185ft (56m) on the return from Branton to Whittingham.

Whittingham Church

River Breamish near Ingram

PUBLIC TRANSPORT

The nearest train station is at Alnmouth, about 11 miles to the east of Whittingham, accessible on quiet lanes via Shilbottle. Bus service 473 from Alnwick to Wooler via Whittingham (see page 97)

TOURIST INFORMATION

ALNWICK
01665 510665

ROTHBURY (SEASONAL)
01669 620887

BIKE SHOPS

None on the route. The nearest is (bike hire and spares only) Spar Supermarket, Main Street, Rothbury. 01669 621338

REFRESHMENTS

Glanton - Queens Head pub, cafe and shop

Powburn - Plough pub, teas served in the garage on the A697

Oak woodland near Eslington

ROUTE INSTRUCTIONS

1   From Whittingham, follow signs for Glanton.
2   After 2 miles, at the T-junction in Glanton, turn left and follow the road round to the right, towards Powburn.
3   Descend to Powburn. At the T-junction with the A697, by the Plough pub, turn left, cross the bridge then turn immediately left.
4   After ¾ mile, at the T-junction, turn left.

5 For a short ride, turn left in Branton. Rejoin at Instruction 9.

6 For Ingram and the National Park Visitor Centre, follow the road through Branton then turn first right just before the power lines. Cross the footbridge over the River Breamish and turn left.

7 Follow this road and signs for Ingram Visitor Centre for 2 miles.

8 Retrace your steps as far as Branton (Route instruction 5), crossing the footbridge over the Breamish. Turn right in the village, signposted 'Whittingham'.

9 After almost 2 miles, turn right at the T-junction.

10 Shortly, ignore the first left turning then (easy to miss) after 2 miles, on a sharp right-hand bend, turn left towards 'Eslington, Whittingham'. Shortly, at the T-junction, turn left again.

11 Go past Eslington Park and at the T-junction, bear left to return to Whittingham.

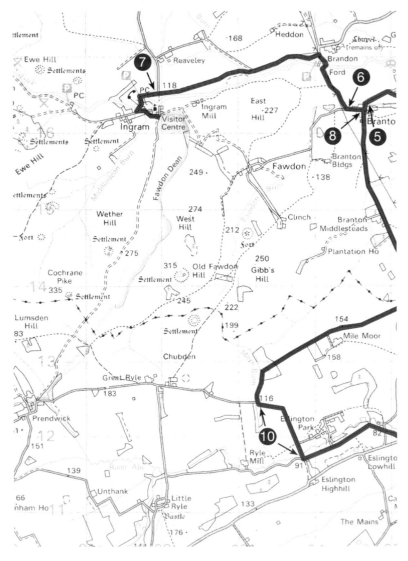

Cheviot foothillls near Ingram

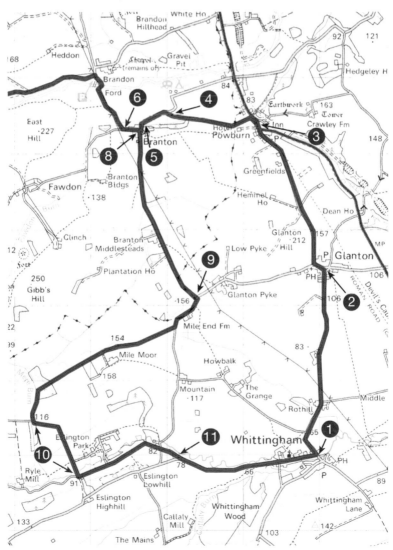

8 Wooler to Chillingham and Chatton

This fine ride starts from Wooler which, despite its compact size, is the largest settlement between Alnwick and Berwick, giving an indication of how sparsely populated the area is. The Pennine Cycleway is followed south before turning east off the waymarked route, onto a stone track and a footbridge crossing of Wooler Water at Haugh Head. The ride runs through lovely countryside of beech and pine and rolling pasture fields, with distant hills on the far side of the River Till valley. Expect to see lots of pheasants and perhaps a red squirrel. You may wish to visit Chillingham Castle or the pub in Chatton - this is your only chance of refreshments along the way. More quiet lanes are used past the big stone farmhouses at Hetton and Horton before recrossing the Till and returning to Wooler.

STARTING POINT AND DISTANCE
Cheviot Street, Wooler
22 miles

GRADE OF DIFFICULTY
Moderate

MAJOR CLIMBS
There are several short 60-130ft (20-40m) climbs on this undulating ride, plus two more notable ascents:

1   A 230ft (70m) climb at the start of the ride south from Wooler.

2   A long, steady 330ft (100m) climb from the River Till north of Chatton to the Lowick road.

Rich arable fields near Wooler

Chillingham Castle entrance

PUBLIC TRANSPORT

No train station nearby (the nearest is at Berwick). Bus service 473 from Alnwick to Wooler via Whittingham (see page 97)

TOURIST INFORMATION

WOOLER (SEASONAL)

01668 282123

BIKE SHOPS

FERGUSONS MOTORS AND CYCLES

Haugh Head Garage, South Road, Wooler (on route next to instruction 3). Also does bike hire. 01668 281316

REFRESHMENTS

Wooler - lots of choice

Chatton - Percy Arms pub, village shop also does teas.

ROUTE INSTRUCTIONS

1   Leave Wooler on Cheviot Street by the Anchor Inn and the Bank of Scotland, following 'Pennine Cycleway' signs southbound.

2   Easy to miss. After almost 2 miles, at the point where the power lines are almost overhead, opposite a road on the right, turn left downhill on a wide stone track, signposted 'Unsuitable for motors ½ mile ahead'.

3   Go downhill and cross a bumpy bridge. At the T-junction with the A697, turn left then first right, signposted 'Lilburn Hill ¾'.

4   Follow the road for 2 miles past farms and round a sharp left-hand bend at the bottom of the hill. At a T-junction on a sharp bend, bear right (in effect, go straight ahead).

5   Cross the bridge and turn left, signposted 'Alnwick, Eglingham'. Climb to the top of the hill, follow the road around a sharp left-hand bend by a house (there is a bridleway and a concrete track ahead).

6   Easy to miss. At the bottom of the hill turn left by a cluster of stone barns.

7   Go through the ford (or over the footbridge) and climb past the tower on the left. At the T-junction turn right, signposted 'Chillingham, Alnwick' then, after 1 mile, at the T-junction by the gates to Chillingham Castle, turn left, signposted 'Chillingham, Chatton'.

8   After almost 3 miles, at the T-junction with the B6348 in Chatton, turn right, signposted 'Belford, Bamburgh'. Go past the Percy Arms pub and turn left, signposted 'Lowick, Berwick'.

9   After 1½ miles, at the crossroads by a Give Way sign, go straight ahead (no sign) past a telephone box.

10 After almost 2 miles, ignore a right turn to Belford. Follow signs for Holburn and Berwick then, shortly, take the next left, signposted 'Hetton Hall, Doddington'.

11 Long steady climb. After 2½ miles, at the crossroads by a Give Way sign turn left, signposted 'Horton, Wooler'.

12 After 2¼ miles at the T-junction in Horton, with a row of cottages ahead, turn right, signposted 'Weetwood, Doddington, Wooler'.

13 Follow this lane for 1 ½ miles, cross the old stone bridge, and at the T-junction with the B6348 turn right, signposted 'Wooler, Route 68'.

14 After 2 miles, at the crossroads with the A697, go straight ahead up Church Street to return to the start.

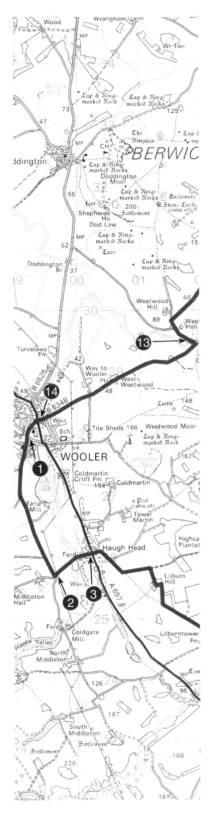

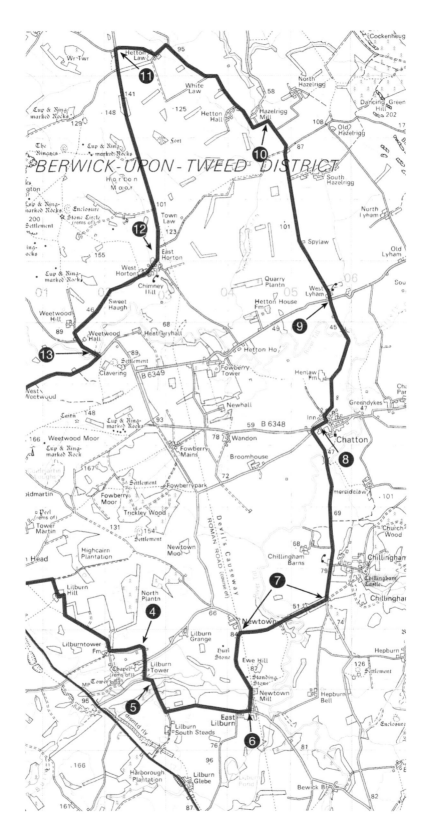

9 Around the Kyloe Hills
north of Belford

Soon after leaving Belford, views open up to the North Sea and ahead to the Holy Island of Lindisfarne. The ride uses the course of the old A1; you can see and hear the new A1, along with the East Coast mainline railway, running parallel and closer to the coast. The ride runs across a landscape of mixed arable and pasture fields, bounded by scraggly hedges, stone walls and dotted with neat stone barns. The climb from Fenwick takes you past a squat, handsome church at the northern end of the Kyloe Hills, with some fine views back to the coast. As you turn south, you swap views of the sea for views of the Cheviot Hills to the east. Hundreds of pheasants appear in the fields, oblivious to the occasional roaring jet on a sortie from RAF Boulmer. You may wish to divert to St Cuthbert's Cave, set in the rocks above Holburn Grange. Notice the carefully-pruned trees and newly-planted hedgerows – an indication that the local estate is taking a real interest in its guardianship of the countryside. The final climb offers the two predominant views of the ride - first towards the Cheviots then, after the summit, out to sea. You finish with a long and exhilarating descent into Belford.

Wide open country south of Lowick

Northumberland day ride

STARTING POINT AND DISTANCE
Blue Bell Hotel, Belford
17 miles

GRADE OF DIFFICULTY
Moderate

MAJOR CLIMBS
1   There is a short, 130ft (40m) climb at the start from Belford. then two more 130ft (40m) climbs either side of Fenwick.
2   On the way back, there is a 220ft (67m) climb between the B6253 and Holburn.
3   The last and longest climb of 395ft (120m) onto Belford Moor follows the minor road between Dancing Green Hill and Bowden Doors.

PUBLIC TRANSPORT
The nearest railway station is at Berwick, about 12 miles north of the northernmost point of the ride. There are various bus services to Belford. Traveline 0870 608 2608

TOURIST INFORMATION
BERWICK
01289 330733

ADDERSTONE, NEAR BELFORD
01668 213678

BIKE SHOPS
The nearest are in Berwick and Wooler:

TWEED CYCLES
(Also cycle hire)
17a Bridge Street
01289 331476

FERGUSONS MOTORS AND CYCLES
(Also cycle hire)
Haugh Head Garage, South Road, Wooler.
01668 281316

REFRESHMENTS
Belford - Blue Bell Hotel, Black Swan pub, several stores

There is a pub in **Lowick**, about 2 miles off the northernmost point of the route

ROUTE INSTRUCTIONS

1 From the Blue Bell Hotel in the centre of Belford, turn left uphill to follow the Route 1 northbound (towards Berwick).

2 Short, steep climb. After 2 miles, with the A1 in sight, turn left, signposted 'Detchant, Route 1'.

3 Climb into Detchant and turn right opposite the telephone box, signposted 'Route 1'.

4 After 3 miles, at the T-junction by a 'Give Way' sign, turn left, signposted 'Route 1'.

5 This ride leaves Route 1 (which bears off to the right). After 1 mile, go past a church at the top of the hill then, after a further mile, turn left at the crossroads at the bottom of the hill, signposted 'Chatton 8'.

6 After 3 ½ miles, if you wish to visit St Cuthbert's Cave (after Holburn), turn left (it is signposted).

7 Easy to miss. After a further 1 ¾ miles, and shortly after passing the lane to North Hazelrigg to the left, take the next left on a sharp right-hand bend, signposted 'Belford 4 ¼'.

8 After 2 miles, at the T-junction by a 'Give Way' sign, turn left, signposted 'Belford 2'. A great descent to finish back in Belford.

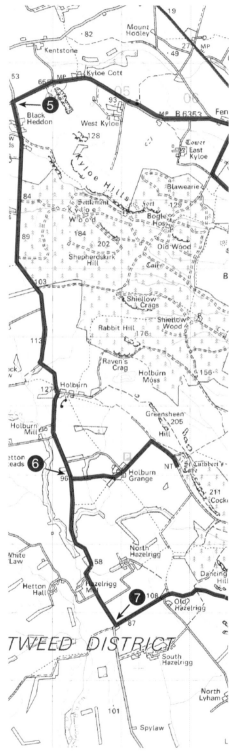

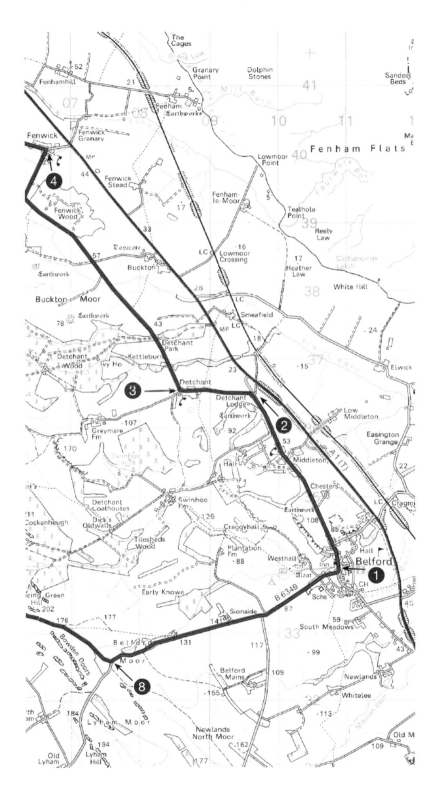

10   Belford to Chatton

Chatton Village and The Percy Arms public house in Chatton

Two of the real highlights of this ride are the views at the top of the long climbs, one at the start and one in the middle. The first, out of Belford, takes you to just over half way to Chatton, where there are panoramic views of the Cheviots to the south-west. Chatton is an attractive stone-built village with a pub and a village shop. Chillingham Castle is famous for its wild cattle, which roam in the parkland on the hill above. Not far from here, you face the tough climb to Ros Castle, which is rewarded with some of the best views in Northumberland. This road has a 'roof-of-the-world' feel, and the occasional gate means that traffic is absolutely minimal. After an undulating stretch, the lane plunges to the A1, with a safe crossing through an underpass. There are two good pubs, one in the attractive red-tiled village of Ellingham with its fine church and hall, the other in Lucker, a few miles further on. A gentle climb back to Belford follows the crossing of Waren Burn just north of Lucker.

STARTING POINT AND DISTANCE
Blue Bell Hotel, Belford
27 miles

GRADE OF DIFFICULTY
Moderate / strenuous

MAJOR CLIMBS
1   There is a climb of 425ft (130m) from the start in Belford to the high point above Chatton.

2   The 650ft (200m) climb from the crossing of the River Till to the south of Chatton starts gently then becomes very steep on its way to Ros Castle.

PUBLIC TRANSPORT
There is a very restricted train service to Chathill station, about 2 miles east of the route at Ellingham. Belford is about 17

Statue of Viscount Hugh Gough at Chillingham.

miles south of Berwick, which has a regular train service.
There are bus services to Belford. Call 0870 608 2608 for details.

TOURIST INFORMATION

ADDERSTONE
on the A1 to the south of Belford
01668 213678

BIKE SHOPS
The nearest are in Berwick and Wooler:

TWEED CYCLES
(Bike hire available)
17a Bridge Street
01289 331476

FERGUSONS MOTORS AND CYCLES
(Bike hire available)
Haugh Head Garage, South Road, Wooler.
01668 281316

REFRESHMENTS
Belford - Blue Bell Hotel, Black Swan pub, stores

Chatton - Percy Arms pub, stores
North Charlton - Masons Arms (just north of the route)
Ellingham - Pack Horse pub
Lucker - Apple pub

ROUTE INSTRUCTIONS
1   From the main square in Belford, take the B6349 towards Wooler. From the end of the village, climb for ½ mile, then turn first left, signposted 'Chatton 5'. Climb to the summit, then descend.
2   After 3 miles, turn right at the T-junction at the bottom of the descent, signposted 'Chatton, Wooler'.
3   Descend into Chatton then, towards the far end of the village, turn left, signposted 'Chillingham'.
4   After 2 miles, go past Chillingham Castle then, after a further mile, take the next left, signposted 'Hepburn'. Steady

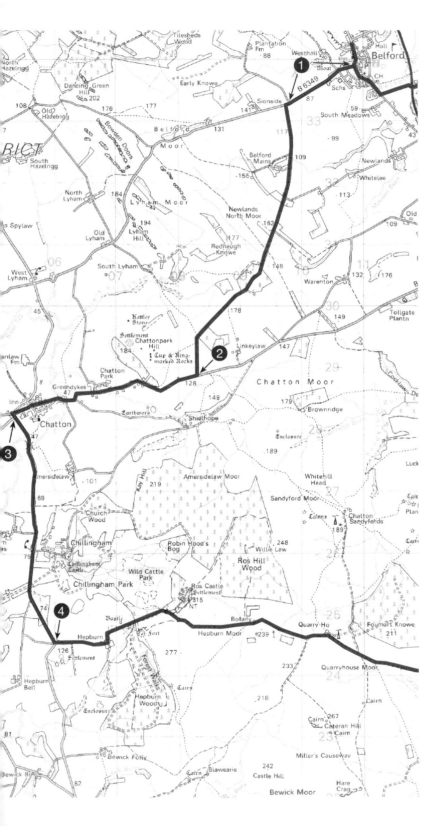

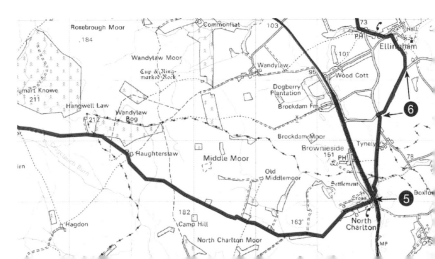

then very steep climb to the summit.

5   Follow this wonderful unfenced road for 7 miles. At the bottom of the final descent, immediately before the A1, turn left onto a lane parallel with the main road, then bear right downhill after 20 yds to go through the subway. Turn left at the end.

6   At the crossroads, turn right, signposted 'Preston, Chathill'. After ¾ mile, take the next left, signposted 'Ellingham', then first right to go past the Pack Horse pub.

7   After ½ mile, at the T-junction, turn left, signposted 'Trunk Road A1' then shortly first right (no sign). Follow this gated and unfenced road.

8   After 1 ½ miles, at the crossroads, go straight ahead, signposted 'Lucker 1 ¼'.

9   This instruction sounds more complicated than it is! At the T-junction by the war memorial, just after the Apple Inn, bear right (in effect straight ahead). At the next T-junction, which follows shortly, bear left (in effect straight ahead). Bear right at the next left-hand bend (in effect straight ahead).

10   At the crossroads following soon, turn right, signposted 'Bradford'.

11   After almost 2 miles, at the T-junction by the windmill, turn sharp left then, after a short distance, bear left onto the B1342.

12   After 2 miles, at the crossroads with the A1, go straight ahead (take care) to return to the centre of Belford.

Entrance to Chillingham Castle

Woodland near Chillingham

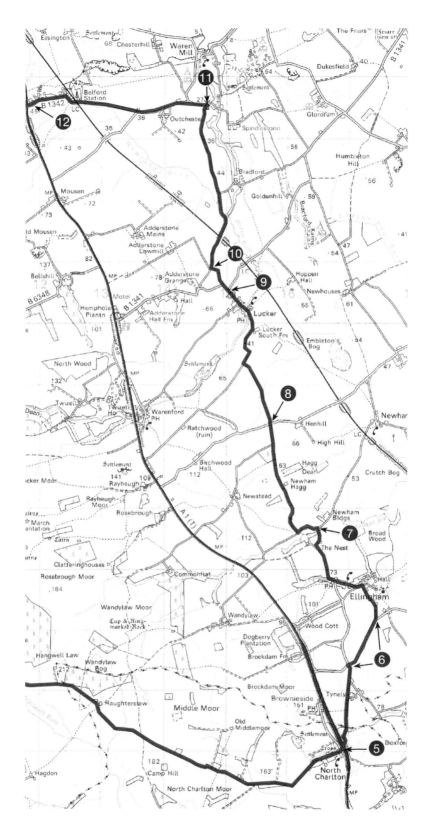

11 Warkworth, Amble and Druridge Bay

The real joy of this ride doesn't become apparent until the second half – when you reach the coast at Druridge – so don't despair as you ride past the Young Offenders' Institution south of Acklington then see the huge crane of the opencast mine against the skyline... Northumberland's true beauty is waiting for you on the coast! The ride starts by heading west from Warkworth on quiet lanes north of the River Coquet valley, crossing the river by the remains of the priory at Brainshaugh. Acklington and Broomhill are the least exciting parts, but the vast sandy beach of Druridge Bay, running for miles in either direction, is worth it. The excellent Druridge Bay Visitor Centre also has fascinating displays, and a good cafe. Amble harbour is another delight, with brightly- coloured fishing boats lining the dock. Finally, the dramatic ruins of Warkworth Castle reward your last climb, at the top of Warkworth's wide and handsome main street.

Cycling along the river with Warkworth Castle in the distance (and inset)

STARTING POINT AND DISTANCE
Centre of Warkworth
Full route - 18 miles
Short route - 11 miles

GRADE OF DIFFICULTY
Easy

MAJOR CLIMBS
None

PUBLIC TRANSPORT
The nearest train station is at
Alnmouth, about 5 miles to the
north of Warkworth along quiet
lanes.
For details of bus services contact
Traveline 0870 608 2 608

TOURIST INFORMATION

AMBLE (SEASONAL)
01665 712313

ALNWICK
01665 510665

BIKE SHOPS

BREEZE'S BIKES
(also cycle hire)
Coquet Street, Amble
01665 710323

REFRESHMENTS
Warkworth - lots of choice
Broomhill - Druridge Bay Inn
Druridge Bay Visitor Centre -
  cafe
Amble - lots of choice

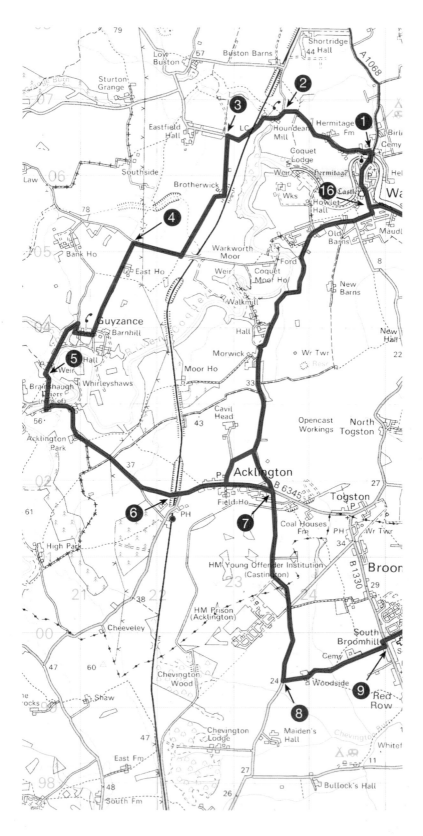

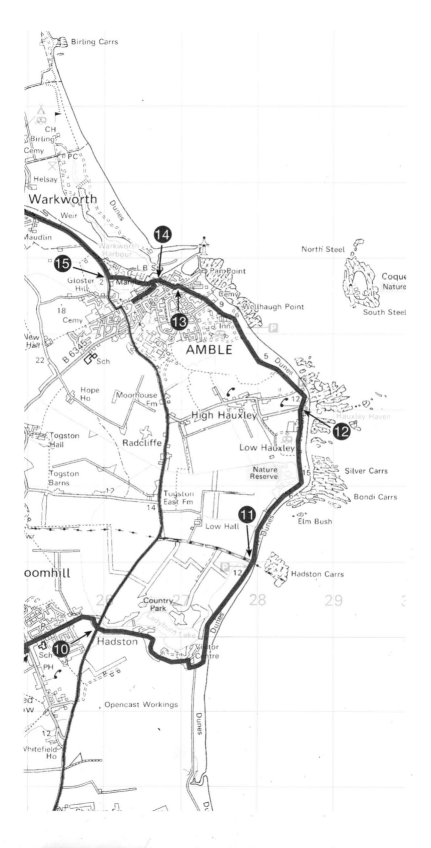

Amble Marina

Woodland lanes near Guyzance

ROUTE INSTRUCTIONS

1 From the centre of Warkworth follow the A1068 north towards Alnwick, cross the bridge over the river and take the first left signposted 'Route 1'.

2 After 1 mile, ignore the turning on the right signposted 'Route 1, Alnmouth'. Continue straight ahead, signposted 'Shilbottle'.

3 Shortly, cross the level crossing then turn first left, signposted 'Brotherwick, Guyzance'.

4 After 1 ½ miles follow the road round a sharp right-hand bend where a road comes in from the left, then shortly turn left at the signpost.

5 Follow the road downhill round a left hairpin bend, following signs for 'Acklington' and 'Felton'. After ½ mile, at the T-junction by a Give Way sign, bear left (in effect, go straight ahead), signposted 'Acklington'. Cross the bridge.

6 After 1 ½ miles, at the T-junction after the railway bridge by a Give Way sign, bear left (in effect go straight ahead) onto the B6345 through Acklington.

SHORT CUT

Turn first left in Acklington, signposted 'Warkworth, Morwick' and follow this road for 3 miles back to Warkworth. At the T-junction at the end of Guilden Road, turn right then shortly left to return to the start.

7 (Main route) At the end of the village of Acklington turn right, signposted 'HM Prison Acklington'.

8 After 1 mile, ignore the first left to Broomhill (opposite the end of the prison). After a further ¾ mile take the next left, signposted 'Broomhill, Woodside'.

9 At the T-junction with the B1330 in Broomhill turn left (no sign) then first right, signposted 'Hadston'.

10 About 100 yards before the main road turn right, passing through a gate onto a tarmac track, signposted 'Public Bridleway'. At the main road go straight ahead, signposted 'Druridge Bay Country Park'. Stay on the road. After 1 mile you will come to Druridge Bay Visitor Centre. Stop here to visit Druridge Bay and admire the coastal views. Take one of the many paths through the dunes onto the beach.

11 The tarmac ends after a further 1 ½ miles. Continue straight ahead, signposted 'Public Bridleway. Low Hauxley'.

12 The path turns back to tarmac. At the T-junction bear right (past a telephone box), signposted 'Route 1, Amble'.

13 Go past the Granary pub, a caravan site and a spire monument in the graveyard. Shortly after passing the Co-op in Amble take the next right, signposted 'Harbour, Parking'.

14 Turn right through the car park after the docks to stay close to the perimeter wall of the marina on a track through the grassy area known locally as 'The Braid'. Join the marina access road by the waterside and bear left.

15 Just before the A1068 turn right alongside the road on an excellent, broad, smooth track, which becomes a narrower, shared-use pavement.

16 At the T-junction at the top of the climb turn right. Follow the A1068 down to Warkworth.

Maps to accompany this guide

ORDNANCE SURVEY LANDRANGER MAP SERIES

75 Berwick-Upon-Tweed Holy Island & Wooler

80 Cheviot Hills & Kielder Water

81 Alnwick & Morpeth, Rothbury & Amble

86 Haltwhistle & Brampton, Bewcastle & Alston

87 Hexham & Haltwhistle

88 Newcastle Upon Tyne, Durham & Sunderland

Available from Ordnance Survey, Sustrans and map / book shops priced £5.99.

Ordnance Survey

Map orders: 0845 200 2712 (or +44 1233 211108 outside UK) or visit the website: www.ordnancesurvey.co.uk

National Cycle Network Map Series

Pennine Cycleway (North) Cycle Route Map

Coast & Castles Cycle Route Map

Hadrian's Cycleway Route Map (available 2005)

Sustrans

These maps are available from Sustrans priced £5.95

www.sustransshop.co.uk or call 0845 113 0065

For details of other cycling maps and publications covering the Northumberland area, contact Sustrans North: 0191 261 6160 or the National Cycle Network Public Information Line: 0845 113 0065

Local public transport

RAIL OPERATORS

Once in the region contact

Arriva Trains

0870 602 3322

www.rrne.co.uk

LOCAL TRAIN SERVICES

Tyne Valley Line (Newcastle – Hexham – Haltwhistle – Carlisle)

East Coast (Morpeth - Newcastle – some services to Alnmouth and Chathill)

East Coast Main Line (Newcastle – Alnmouth – Berwick upon Tweed) services are operated by GNER, Virgin or Arriva Trains Northern. Details from National Rail Enquiries opposite.

LOCAL BUS ROUTES

Some local bus services offer Cycle Carriage (often seasonal – please phone to check before travel):

Hadrian's Wall Bus (Newcastle - Hexham - Carlisle Service) 01434 322002

Kielder Bus summer service (Newcastle - Kielder) Arriva 0191 281 1313 / 01670 812 352

Hexham – Bellingham Tyne Valley Coaches 01434 602217

888 Bus Service (Newcastle - Hexham - Alston - Penrith - Keswick) 01434 381200

For timetable information contact:
Travel Line North East
0870 608 2608
www.jplanner.org.uk

For up to date information on bus services that carry cycles contact:
Travel Line North East
0870 608 2608
www.jplanner.org.uk
www.traveline.org.uk
www.traveline-northeast.co.uk
Northumberland County Council Public Transport Helpline
01670 533128
www.northumberland.gov.uk/vg/cypublic.html

A booklet 'Experience Northumberland by Bus', useful leaflets and timetables can be downloaded from
www.northumberland.gov.uk/services/publications.htm

PRIVATE HIRE

Some parts of Northumberland are not easily accessible by public transport, in which case you might want to consider getting a group together and paying for a private hire service.

Stanley Taxis offer a private service for groups of cyclists (Minibus & Trailer - space for up to 24 bikes) 01207 237 424

Some packaged holiday operators offer transport of bikes, riders and luggage and 'rescue services' – see listings pg 126.

BY TRAIN WITH YOUR BIKE

A minimum of 2 bikes can usually be carried on train services. Reservations are usually unnecessary on local services operated by Arriva Trains Northern (cycles are carried on a first come first served basis), but reservations are required on services operated by GNER, Virgin and other long distance services. You can make a reservation for your bike at the ticket office prior to departure or by phoning National Rail.

National Rail Enquiries 08457 484950
www.nationalrail.co.uk
Network Rail
www.networkrail.co.uk

Package holiday companies

Holiday Lakeland
Dial View, Ireby, Wigton, Cumbria CA7 1EA.
016973 71871 email: hollake@aol.com
www.holiday-lakeland.co.uk
Accommodation book-ahead service, luggage transfer, on-route rescue
and full support service. Offers C2C, Pennine Cycleway North, and Coast
& Castles tours.

Not Entirely Sure Tours
East Farm Croft, Embleton, Alnwick, Northumberland NE66 3XB.
01665 576653 email: enquiries@notentirelysure.co.uk
Cycling breaks, luggage transfer, accommodation. Tour company based in
Northumberland doing cycle tours around north Northumberland

Saddle Skedaddle
Ouseburn Building, Albion Row, East Quayside,
Newcastle upon Tyne NE6 1LL.
0191 265 1110 email: info@skedaddle.co.uk
www.skedaddle.co.uk
Package cycling and activity holidays in UK and abroad.

Tyne Valley Holidays
21 Celandine Close, Gosforth, Newcastle upon Tyne NE3 5JW.
0191 284 7534
Package cycling and walking holidays, cyclists' support services.

Cyclists' support services

Cycle Force
29 Claypath, Durham City DH1 1RH.
0191 384 0319
'Come out and fit it service', cycle hire franchise.

Kielder Bikes Cycle Centre
At Kielder Castle and Hawkhope Centre, Kielder Dam. 01434 250 392
Cycle hire, cyclists' support services – repairs, spares and rescue (Kielder
area).

Stanley Taxis
www.stanleytaxis.co.uk
Full cyclists' support service – rider and bike transport and rescue,
baggage transfer (C2C route, North Pennines, North-East region).
Taxi firm offering drop-off and recovery service
(The Bike Bus) 01207 237 424

Useful websites

Tourist & Visitor Information

Official site for Northumbria - England's North East. Click on 'What to see and do' then 'Activity and special interest holidays' then choose 'Cycling' from the drop-down list.
www.visitnorthumbria.com

North East Listings and directory of businesses and services
www.n-e-life.com

Visitor guide to north Northumberland
www.secretkingdom.com

Coastal section of main circuit
www.northumberland-coast.co.uk

Hadrian's Wall section of main circuit
www.hadrians-wall.org

Pennine Cycleway section of main circuit through Northumberland National Park
www.northumberland-national-park.org.uk

Cycle Route Information

Details of National Cycle Network routes, online maps, information. Follow the links for the North of England.
www.nationalcyclenetwork.org.uk

The definitive guide to the Pennine Cycleway England's longest 'challenge' cycle route.
www.cycle-routes.org/penninecycleway

Excellent site for Hadrian's Cycleway – Sea to Sea the Roman Way!
www.cycle-routes.org/hadrianscycleway/index/html

Accommodation listings and information for the Coast and Castles Cycle Route between Tynemouth and Edinburgh, also has info on the Reivers Cycle Route and the C2C Cycle Route.
www.coast-and-castles.co.uk

The official site for the new w2w (Walney to Wearside) cycle route which is opening in 2005. This route will give a new 'coast to coast' cycling experience via the Lake District, North Pennines, Teesdale and historic Durham. This website will launched by early 2005.
www.cyclingw2w.info

Cycling Maps and Guides

Cycle maps, guides, leaflets and publications ('North of England' section).
www.sustransshop.co.uk

View and buy Ordnance Survey maps for the whole of the UK
www.ordnancesurvey.co.uk

Sells local cycle route maps, guides and books.
www.northumberland.gov.uk/giftshop

Northumberland & Newcastle upon Tyne Cycling Information

The definitive on-line guide to cycling England's North East.
www.cyclenorthumbria.org.uk

Follow links to 'Visitor's Guide', 'Countryside Activities', 'Cycle
Northumberland' pages.
www.northumberland.gov.uk

Information on cycling in Newcastle and Northumberland.
www.tynebikes.org.uk

We hope that you have enjoyed your cycling journey around
Northumberland and discovered wonderful countryside, great local
hospitality and hidden gems never encountered by car borne tourists.

We welcome feedback, so please do get in touch if you have any
comments about this book or have recommendations of your own on
places to stay, visit and go cycling in Northumberland.

Contact Sustrans via the National Cycle Network Information Line
0845 113 0065 or email: info@sustrans.org.uk
Contact Sustrans North East Office (covers the Northumberland area)
0191 261 6160 or email: newcastle@sustrans.org.uk